*Making It*
*in America*

*Making It in America* was prepared
under a grant
from the Weyerhaeuser Foundation

# *Making It in America*

## The Role of Ethnicity in Business Enterprise, Education, and Work Choices

*Edited by*
*M. Mark Stolarik and Murray Friedman*

Lewisburg
Bucknell University Press
London and Toronto: Associated University Presses

Associated University Presses
440 Forsgate Drive
Cranbury, NJ 08512

Associated University Presses
25 Sicilian Avenue
London WC1A 2QH, England

Associated University Presses
2133 Royal Windsor Drive
Unit 1
Mississauga, Ontario
Canada L5J 1K5

The paper used in this publication meets the
requirements of the American National Standard for
Permanence of Paper for Printed Library Materials Z39.48-1984

**Library of Congress Cataloging-in-Publication Data**
Main entry under title:

Making it in America.

Contents: Ethnicity and business enterprise / Ivan
Light—Ethnicity and education / David Hogan—
Ethnicity and the world of work / Milton Cantor—[etc.]
1. Success in business—United States—Addresses,
essays, lectures. 2. Minorities—United States—
Addresses, essays, lectures. 3. Minority business
enterprises—United States—Addresses, essays,
lectures. I. Stolarik, M. Mark, 1943–
II. Friedman, Murray, 1926–
HF5386.M294 1986      338.6′422′0973      84-46100
ISBN 0-8387-5092-3 (alk. paper)

Printed in the United States of America

# Contents

# Introduction

MURRAY FRIEDMAN

The Bronx High School of Science has been justifiably famous for producing students who have come away with National Merit Scholarship awards with great regularity. Over the years, out of perhaps forty such scholarships awarded to its students annually, Jewish students have won between seven and ten. Recently, the school had some seven winners in the Westinghouse Science Talent Search; six of them were Asian students. Since Asians make up only 17 percent of the school's population, one observer has noted, "The swinging elbow that runs the life of New York is still at work."[1]

Although the record of the Bronx High School of Science suggests the importance today of ethnic and cultural factors in "Making It in America," social scientists have tended to see the success or lack of success of minorities and disadvantaged peoples, for the most part, as related to social class. That is to say, the children of those at the lower end of the social scale, who possess less income and education, it is widely believed, tend to sink to the bottom, while the children of those who are more affluent receive economic and other supports that make for advancement in American life.

Closely related to this perception of class has been awareness of racial, religious, and ethnic discrimination. Minority groups over the years have been barred formally or informally from equal access to employment, education, and housing. As a result, their opportunities have been limited. In a classic study, Carey McWilliams referred to anti-Semitism as a mask for privilege.[2] His thesis was that ethnic prejudice of this kind was a device for maintaining the special rights and privileges of upper-class elements of the society.

7

It is also clear, of course, that the ability to achieve success or at least a reasonable standard of living and way of life is closely related to broader social and economic currents, including periods of prosperity and recession. This country's present experience with obsolescent industry and overseas competition are good examples.

In recent years, however, we have become more conscious of the pluralistic character of American life. The civil rights and later race revolutions of the sixties focused public attention on blacks and other racial minorities. Then, in the seventies, we witnessed what Michael Novak called the "rise of the unmeltable ethnics" who were experiencing their own growing sense of identity and group consciousness. In short, to our understanding of class differences and the effects of discrimination, we added the need to understand how the cultural backgrounds of certain groups in society have influenced both the groups themselves and the broader society.

Moreover, with the passage of the immigration reform act in 1965, our already diverse society has seen the arrival of new immigrant streams—from Central and Latin America, Asia, and southern and Eastern Europe. New York, Miami, and many other cities have become increasingly peopled by these new groups. In addition, the 1980 census reports that Mexican-Americans (or Chicanos as they are sometimes called) have become for the first time the largest segment of the minority population in Los Angeles.

This growing diversity, coupled with increasing ethnic and racial consciousness, has led social scientists to look more closely at the nature and impact of group life in America. This has begun to produce a new body of literature that raises questions about many of our conventional beliefs. For example, some ethnic or racial groups, while suffering intense prejudice and disadvantage, manage to overcome these handicaps and even go on to success. Also, we know that some migrants surpass the income of native-born members of their group already in America.

Ivan Light, in his book, *Ethnic Enterprise in America,* and in his conference paper here, has examined how the Koreans, Chinese, Japanese, Jews, and both West Indian and southern-originated blacks have been helped or hindered in their development of a small-business class by the presence or absence within their respective groups of special credit systems, family support systems, and a rich variety of other cultural factors. His work helps explain what is clearly visible to those of us who walk through cities at lunchtime and note the Korean and Vietnamese fruit stands, often operated by men and women with little or no knowledge of the English language, who, somehow, are "making it."

Position in the class structure, exploitation, and discrimination will always be central factors affecting how groups fare in our society. Yet this new body of social science materials and everyday observations suggests that groups can overcome their disadvantages by organizing themselves to draw upon group support systems that have evolved over the years to deal with a hostile environment.

In order to promote greater awareness of the new insights, the Balch Institute For Ethnic Studies and the Philadelphia Chapter of the American Jewish Committee decided to sponsor a conference that on 21 and 22 April 1983 brought experts in the field together with educational and civic leaders to examine the cultural systems of groups. Now by publishing the results of that discussion, we hope to bring the work of the researchers to a wider audience and to expand the circle of dialogue even further. In addressing the ethnic factors that help or inhibit success, however, we do not mean to downplay the forces of deprivation and discrimination and the horrible toll they take on so many people's lives. Moreover, we certainly do not mean to encourage the deplorable notion that there are genetic differences in intelligence among various groups in the population, for we believe that this allegedly "scientific" racism simply places an additional burden on groups who have already been burdened too much by injustice.

Our conference was held during a time of economic recession or depression. In this difficult period, we have been faced with cutbacks in governmental funding that point up more dramatically the need to examine the rich internal resources that enable groups to assist their own members. In short, we believe that the current period literally forces us to understand more about the cultural systems of groups and how they can be utilized more fully to help alleviate or resolve social problems. In their seminal analysis, *To Empower People: The Role of Mediating Structures in Public Policy*, Peter L. Berger and Richard John Neuhaus have traced the history of those intermediate institutions that stand between government and the individual—family, neighborhood, ethnic, racial, and religious groupings. They point out that throughout history, people turned to such sources of support as the major devices in helping them cope with life but that the emergence of the welfare state, in response to a period of rampaging capitalism earlier in the century and later to the Great Depression, tended to weaken the intermediate institutions and force a greater reliance on the role of government. The issue today may be to learn how to use government resources to strengthen and not overwhelm these vital institutions.[3]

In inviting the various experts we have assembled here to present their view on the cultural systems that different groups bring to education, business enterprise, and the world of work, we have made a careful effort to provide diversity of opinion. Among the authors represented here, David Hogan and Milton Cantor have very real reservations about placing a heavy emphasis on cultural factors. They continue to see structural forces as being primary in determining where groups stand in the social scheme of things. Others, including Novak and Light, draw our attention more centrally to the cultural dimension.

The Balch Institute For Ethnic Studies and the Philadelphia Chapter of the American Jewish Committee wish to thank all of these scholars. We take pleasure in presenting their varied viewpoints and the opportunity to open up what we believe to be a relatively new vein of concern, the cultural dimension, in dealing with a wide range of public-policy issues. In doing so we want also to express our appreciation to the Weyerhaeuser Foundation for funding the conference and making possible this publication. It is our hope that through the conference and the book we can stimulate a greater interest in the cultural dimension of the group experience.

## Notes

1. Jimmy Breslin, "Move Over Levine—Make Room For Chiang," *Philadelphia Daily News*, 8 February 1983.

2. Carey McWilliams, *A Mask for Privilege: Anti-Semitism in America* (Boston: Little, Brown & Co., 1948).

3. Peter L. Berger and Richard John Neuhaus, *To Empower People: The Role of Mediating Structures in Public Policy* (Washington: American Enterprise Institute for Public Policy Research, 1977).

*Making It
in America*

# 1

## Ethnicity and Business Enterprise

### Ivan Light

Economists distinguish between entrepreneurs and managers.[1] Managers operate in real markets so the parameters of their decisions are calculable. Entrepreneurs fill gaps in markets, innovate, and make decisions in contexts that are riddled with imponderables and, therefore, with uncertainty. In the paper that follows I treat entrepreneurship as synonymous with business self-employment. Entrepreneurs may employ thousands or head one-man firms. In either case, they take their share out of any residual remaining after their firm's expenses have been met, and are distinguishable in this regard from salaried managers, who, their work completed, become creditors of the business.[2]

Frank Knight long ago declared that "the supply of entrepreneurs in society is one of the chief factors in determining the number and size of its economic units."[3] He was soon challenged, however, by the Austrian economist Joseph Schumpeter.[4] Schumpeter supposed that entrepreneurship was a personality characteristic of the talented virtuosos of economic history but also supposed that entrepreneurship was randomly distributed in every human population in equal proportion.[5] Therefore, like air or water, entrepreneurship was an essential in the economic process, but it could safely be taken for granted.

This is the starting point of discussion, for the current state of our knowledge is the result of successive revisions of Schumpeter's idea. The first critique was empirical. Schumpeter's view depended on armchair speculation, not evidence. However, as soon as scholars inquired into entrepreneurship in historical societies, they learned that rates varied among ethnic and religious

populations. According to Frank Young, entrepreneurs are "located with high frequency in subgroups that have a religious or
ethnic character."[6] This finding was confirmed by McClelland and
Winter, who wrote:

> Wherever economic growth begins, some tiny community can
> nearly always be identified which has played a major entrepre-
> neurial role—such as the Jews or Quakers in parts of the West,
> the Parsis and Jains in India, the Antioquenos in Colombia and
> so forth.[7]

Recent scholarship continues to affirm this point. Describing the
origins of the Industrial Revolution in Britain, Arthur Francis
writes:

> A notable feature of the development of UK industry has been
> the extent to which currently successful firms were founded by
> men from minority groups.[8]

In the social sciences the long-prevailing interpretation held
that intergroup differences in rates of entrepreneurship reflected
intergroup differences in culture. Sociologists, following Max
Weber, stressed the importance of religious values for group
entrepreneurship, while psychologists, following David Mc-
Clelland, stressed a "need for achievement," which groups transmitted differentially to young members.[9] Either way, these social
science interpretations both supposed that individuals first intro-
jected group values, norms, beliefs, and skills, then fanned out in
the world, where they acted out in life what they had learned at
mother's knee. A useful analogy can be found in the mechanical
toys one sometimes sees for sale on urban street corners. Surrounded by his stationary toys, the vendor conveys animation to
each by winding its springs and letting it go. When released, each
toy goes its programmed distance in its programmed manner. But
the moving toys ignore one another. If we think of the vendor as
society and of his toys as the next generation of business owners,
we see society first programming its youth for subsequent business careers, then releasing the young adults to act out their
programmed economic activity independent of one another. In a
sense, all the important action occurs when the machinery is
constructed and the spring wound. Thereafter what happens is
only actualization of latent potentialities built into the mechanism.

This culture and personality approach to entrepreneurship was long the orthodox social science view. However, in the last decade, this orthodoxy has been rejected on the grounds that it is too individualistic and ignores situational pressures.[10] Individualism characterizes the behavior of wind-up toys, but in real life entrepreneurs form groups that combine the disparate resources of individual members, strengthening each and deriving from each one's increased strength greater collective power. For example, if business owners exchange information or conspire in restraint of trade, they have formed an informal group in the course of their economic activity. It cannot be assumed that business owners march away to stand or fall on their individual merits. Sometimes they do; sometimes they do not. This is an empirical matter that should be decided on the basis of evidence. Socialization does occur and it does impart values, motivations, beliefs, and capabilities into young generations, with consequences for that generation's business style. All of that is true as far as it goes. It is, however, necessary to question the old-fashioned assumption that any resulting entrepreneurship is *invariably* individualistic.

A great deal of research has shown that entrepreneurs not only emerge from groups, they function best in groups. Thus, the study of how entrepreneurs are socialized has to yield to the study of how they actually practice their business. In the opinion of Frank Young, entrepreneurship should be studied by examining clusters, not individuals.[11] Young's conclusion is superbly documented by Nathaniel Leff, who has studied the operation of "economic groups" in Latin American industry:

> The group is a multicompany firm which transacts in different markets and does so under common entrepreneurial and financial control. More generally, this pattern of industrial organization has two essential features. First, the group draws its capital and its high-level managers from sources which transcend a single family. . . . Participants are people linked by relations of interpersonal trust, on the basis of similar personal, ethnic, or communal background.[12]

A second objection to the orthodox stress on culture is that it ignores situational pressures. Because of their culturally transmitted values and beliefs, the old view held, individualistic entrepreneurs have a proclivity for self-employment. Wherever settled, they act out this predisposition, which is so powerful it wins out in any circumstances. Of course, such cases do exist. As Marlene Sway's research on gypsies has shown, that group has a catalog of entrepreneurial occupations that it practices equally well in socialist, communist, or capitalist societies. Wherever the gypsies go, crystal balls and tarot cards are their means of livelihood. But there are negative instances too. These instances arise when groups with a supposedly cultural proclivity for entrepreneurship abruptly reduce their entrepreneurship or, conversely, when groups with a supposedly low proclivity abruptly increase it. British Quakers provide an example of the first type. During the Industrial Revolution, Quakers were heavily overrepresented in the pioneer industries of steam and water frame technology. But industrial self-employment is no longer characteristic of British Quakers and has not been for a century. Conversely, a generation ago, Koreans had a worldwide reputation for commercial backwardness, in marked contrast to the Japanese, and anthropologists located the cause in Korean culture. Even so, in the last decade Korea's rate of economic growth has been among the highest in the world.[13] Why the changes? Quaker and Korean values and beliefs have lingered—and a constant cannot explain a change. Rather, it is reasonable to suppose that while the groups' cultural heritages retained their characteristic features, external situations changed—thus calling out behavioral adaptation suppressed under previous conditions.[14]

Of all the situational pressures affecting entrepreneurship, socioeconomic disadvantage is most important. Disadvantaged in the labor market by social or religious discrimination, minority groups derive a motive for self-employment regardless of their cultural heritage. Thus, when Quakers were subject to discrimination in Britain, they embraced business, and when social disadvantage disappeared, Quakers lost their interest in business. In the same sense, Korean entrepreneurship in the United States is largely explained by the immigrant's unfamiliarity with English. Unable to speak English, Koreans cannot get good jobs, so they choose business self-employment over dead-end work.[15] In these cases Quakers or Koreans are entrepreneurial or not entrepreneurial in pretty strict correspondence to how disadvantaged they are in the wage labor force.

Putting these issues together, we generate a foursquare tabulation (table 1) that roughly summarizes current thinking about

Table 1

Group Resources and Labor Force Disadvantage as
Co-Determinants of Rate of Entrepreneurship

| | Group Resources | |
| --- | :---: | :---: |
| | Many | None |
| Labor Force Disadvantage | | |
| Much | +, + | −, + |
| None | +, + | −, − |

ethnic entrepreneurship. Groups can be disadvantaged or not and they can have cultural resources or lack them. The most entrepreneurial are the disadvantaged groups with resources. The least are the non-disadvantaged groups lacking resources. Other cases fall between. One difference between this foursquare table and the orthodox social science view is that the latter explained intergroup rates of entrepreneurship on the basis of cultural resources alone, whereas the revised view accommodates situational factors as well.

## Entrepreneurship in Practice

At this point I wish to illustrate how ethnicity interacts with entrepreneurship by citing concrete examples that my coworker Edna Bonacich (University of California, Riverside) and I have uncovered in a lengthy research into Korean entrepreneurship in Los Angeles. Here, a list Peter Kilby compiled of the thirteen functions of entrepreneurship will provide headings under which I will classify and explain what the Koreans do.[16]

### 1. Perception of Market Opportunities (Novel or Imitative)

Korean entrepreneurs cluster heavily in specific small-business industries, and we found that their newspapers contain two-thirds as many listings of business opportunities as the *Los Angeles times,* even though Koreans are only 1 percent of the Los Angeles population. Additionally, 50 percent of the opportunities listed in the Korean press come under categories that account for only 10 percent of listings in the *Los Angeles Times.* In other words,

Koreans exchange information about business opportunities, and just being able to read Korean permits one to share this information without transmitting it to those who cannot read want ads in Korean.

## 2. Gaining Command over Scarce Resources

Land, labor, and capital are scarce resources, but the formation of Koreatown as an ethnic neighborhood has given the immigrant minority a concentration point where those scarce resources are availalbe to Korean entrepreneurs under terms that minimize both market costs and language barriers. Even Korean firms located elsewhere benefit from brokerage institutions located in Koreatown. In fact, thanks to Koreatown, it is in many respects easier to operate a small business in Los Angeles if one is Korean-speaking than if one is English-speaking because the English-speaking people do not have any comparable center wherein radiating lines of influence concentrate.

## 3. Purchasing Inputs

Although Koreans pay the market price for most inputs, they pay less than the market price for at least some of the inputs, such as raw materials that they acquire from other Koreans and from South Korea. Getting an occasional break or a discount helps Korean merchants survive the competition.

## 4. Responding to Competition

Koreans have formed Korean trade associations in some of the industries (including garment) in which they participate heavily. At present these are not particularly influential, but there is a desire for expanded influence. The Korean press also alerts readers to economic threats arising from outside competitors, and Korean social and political institutions take an interest in these issues as well.

As a result of ethnic clustering, however, Koreans find internal competition among Koreans a more severe problem than competition with non-Koreans even though internal competition comes up against ethnic solidarity and Korean efforts to deal with the matter. Korean newspapers publicize the problem and encourage coethnics to combine against mutual destruction. Insofar as anything can be done to restrain internal competition, the solidarity of the Korean community is the critical resource.

## 5. Dealing with the Public Bureaucracy

Two illustrations expose the importance of ethnic connections here. First, Korean merchants, facing a serious crime problem in central Los Angeles, raised a concerted outcry that compelled the city to allocate more police to Korean neighborhoods, In addition, the Koreans voluntarily subscribed the money to pay for a police substation, which has made Koreatown a safer and more attractive place to do business.

In the second case, in November 1982 the city of Los Angeles unveiled a freeway sign marking the Koreatown exit from the Santa Monica freeway. The sign, which directs business to Koreatown, was put in place because city politicians appreciated the money Korean merchants have channeled into their reelection campaigns.

## 6. Management of Human Relations with the Firm

Most Korean firms are small, and for them "human relations" are really just family affairs. However, even if Korean firms hire nonkin coethnics, their work force responds to nationalistic appeals based on common ethnicity: "We Koreans must hang together or we won't make it in Los Angeles."

## 7. Management of Customer Relations

Koreans in Los Angeles (as in Philadelphia and New York) have experienced social tension with black customers who resent their presence in black residential areas. To deal with the problem the Korean Association of Southern California signed an intercommunal "treaty" of mutual assistance with the Watts Labor Community Action Committee representing the black community on the other side. Here the ethnic association used its good offices for the management and reduction of intergroup tension, benefiting its own members but not outside competitors.

## 8. Financial Management

Koreans exchange financial assistance informally, using devices such as a rotating credit association. Likewise, Korean accountants offer their service in the Korean language, as do Korean banks, while nearby American banks and accounting firms have added "Korean-speaking divisions" staffed, of course, by Koreans. Mutual trust based on common ethnicity reinforces the Korean community's ability to deploy its money wisely and with safety.

## 9. Production Management

Korean garment contractors compare notes on factory management, and we suppose these communications provide a kind of school for sewing entrepreneurs. The various institutions of the Korean community also offer Korean-speaking persons management services and educational programs that are publicized in the ethnic press.

## 10. Acquiring and Overseeing Assembly of Factories

We found very great homogeneity in business purchases. For instance, Hollywood Koreans sold their liquor licenses to co-ethnics in 79 percent of such transactions even though fellow Koreans were only 15 percent of the city's license buyers. This mechanism presumably carries over to the sewing factories, wig businesses, grocery stores, and other Korean industries. Operating within the Korean-language community is easier and cheaper than operating in the general marketplace. Koreans only ventured into the general marketplace when they could not find a coethnic seller.

## 11. Industrial Engineering

No data.

## 12. Upgrading Product Quality

Because Koreans work harder than non-Koreans, Korean firms can produce a better product or service for less money than do competitors.

*13. Technical and Product Innovation*

We have no evidence that Korean entrepreneurs invent new techniques or products in greater proportion than non-Koreans. On the other hand, ethnic lines of communication guarantee that Korean firms pick up new techniques and products rapidly. Once a Korean firm on the circuit has accepted an innovation, news travels quickly to the others. In this case ethnic links double as communication networks. Of course, this tendency is enhanced by the clustering of Koreans in particular industrial niches so that many Koreans share a common industrial background and common concerns.

## Real and Spurious Contributions of Ethnicity to Entrepreneurship

Having argued and demonstrated that ethnicity confers resources that facilitate entrepreneurship, I now must distinguish between real and spuriously ethnic resources, on the one hand, and between productive and nonproductive resources, on the other. Real ethnic resources derive from the social identification people make with an ethnic or immigrant community. Spurious ethnic resources are connected with the aforesaid people but do not require or result from identification with a community. Productive resources are those ethnic or nonethnic resources that contribute to the efficiency of firms and indirectly to profitability. Nonproductive resources are those that contribute directly to the profitability of firms without necessarily enhancing efficiency. Table 2 represents my distinctions in a four-square format for ease of exposition.

The upper-left square represents the productive ethnic resources. Ethnic heritages can be productive when they contain values, motivations, skills, institutions, beliefs, and attitudes conducive to economic efficiency. For example, I have argued elsewhere that Japanese and Chinese rotating credit associations were intact cultural transfers that facilitated pre–World War II Asian business enterprise.[17] Similarly, Jarvenpa and Zenner found that Scots traders in northern Canada carried over the Atlantic a high value on personal thrift that was of obvious utility in Scots firms.[18] In these two cases idiosyncratic ethnic values and

Table 2
Ethnic Resources and Productive Resources

|  | Ethnic | Nonethnic |
|---|---|---|
| Productive | Heritages | Class Resources |
|  | Solidarity | Labor Force Disadvantage |
|  | Communication | Hostile Stereotypes |
| Nonproductive | Restraint of Trade |  |
|  | Vertical Integration | Labor Law Evasion |
|  | Organized Crime | Tax Evasion |

institutions produced resources that encouraged entrepreneurship. Ethnic heritages have to be appraised item by
item for their compatibility with entrepreneurship. Rarely do we
confront cases of total compatibility or total incompatibility, but it
is reasonable to suppose that some ethnic heritages are more
compatible with entrepreneurship than others.

Whatever its origin, ethnic solidarity confers another class of
productive resources that encourage entrepreneurship. First, solidarity enhances intragroup communication. In turn, communication enhances transfer of knowledge, rapid and effective
deployment of labor and capital, technical competence, labor
recruitment and training, marketing sophistication, and access to
support skills. Describing "economic groups" in Latin America,
Nathaniel Leff has noted:

> The group's internal relations of interpersonal trust permit the
> formation of larger top management teams than would other-
> wise be possible. This facilitates effective communication of
> authority and enables firms to overcome organizational con-
> straints on size and efficiency.[19]

Second, solidarity increases mutual trust within the ingroup. In
turn, mutual trust relaxes credit barriers and provides loan guar-
antors, while reducing theft, police effort, and suspicion. The
process is well illustrated in Roland Robinson's empirical account
of how small businesses in the United States are actually financed:

> A prospective entrepreneur . . . canvasses first his own means,
> then those of his friends and neighbors, and finally more re-
> mote relatives. If he is a man well regarded by friends and

neighbors, he may be able to secure supporting financing from them.[20]

In a situation of this sort, an entrepreneur embedded in social groups obtains capital on favorable terms simply because of his social embeddedness.

Finally, ethnic solidarity promotes self-discipline and hard work. In many cases, intergroup business competition furnishes motivation by equating success of the ethnic firm with success of the ethnic group: "They call us gooks, but we'll prove we're as good as they are." Therefore, the firm's performance can draw upon motivational resources unavailable to nonethnic firms. Additionally, to reflect well upon their group, individuals strive to excel while avoiding disgraceful acts that would stain the reputation of their community. In a very general but pervasive manner, the ideal of ethnic honor produces the disciplined work habits that support the economic viability of ethnic firms. As Abner Cohen has written of the Hausa minority in Ibadan, Nigeria:

> Its members form a moral community which constrains the behavior of the individual, and insures a large measure of conformity with common values and principles.[21]

The lower-left square (table 2) represents nonproductive resources derived from ethnic identification. The first is restraint of trade. When coethnics pile up in and tend to dominate an industry, they are well positioned to utilize ethnic solidarity for price fixing.[22] Naturally this tendency toward the formation of cartels encounters contradictory pressures from market forces—but insofar as ethnicity is both salient and pronounced, its banner provides a rallying point around which business competitors can assemble for anticompetitive association. Cartels are profitable for the participants but not because they augment the productivity of ethnic firms.

A related restraint is vertical integration. Indeed, the typical progression of ethnics is radial expansion from a core into kindred lines. For example, Italians in San Francisco started as fishermen, then opened in turn fish markets, seafood restaurants, and restaurant supply houses, thus squeezing every dollar out of the Bay City's fishing industry. Such vertical integration provides leverage not only to restrain competition internally but also to restrain external competition as well by excluding outsiders from an industry. Although restraint of competition may or may not augment efficiency, it invariably augments profits.

When voluntary restraint is ineffective, as it often is, ethnic concentration in small business unavoidably increases internal competition. In this situation, history offers some instances in which organized crime has imposed involuntary restraints of trade in the ostensible interests of regulating destructive competition. The racketeer Maxie Eisen imposed this kind of competitive truce upon the kosher poultry industry in Chicago during the 1920s, and Chinese tongs once had a hand in regulating competition in Chinatown trades.[23]

The upper-right square (table 2) describes productive resources that are nonethnic in origin but are frequently confused with ethnic resources. These are, first of all, class resources, such as money and education. Naturally people whose socioeconomic status affords them more money and education fare better in business than people with less, and Cubans in Miami and Koreans in Los Angeles are cases in point. These entrepreneurial immigrants entered the United States with educational backgrounds and bank accounts much in excess of the common-man level in this country, let alone in their country of origin. Since the immigrant populations of these nationalities are skewed toward higher socioeconomic strata, the immigrants' entrepreneurship seems ethnic—whereas a substantial contribution was actually made by the class resources they brought. Of course, class resources and ethnic resources can combine; they need not exclude one another.[24] But it is well to separate the two analytically in order to avoid confusing what has been contributed to entrepreneurship by ethnicity and what has been furnished by inherited wealth and social position.[25]

Labor force disadvantage compels ethnics to scramble for a living in self-employment. Facing a hard choice between unemployment and self-employment, immigrants and ethnics must accomplish whatever is necessary to become and remain self-employed. Strictly speaking, this pressure does not derive from ethnicity, but it does confer competitive advantages upon ethnics, as people disadvantaged in the labor market may club together on the basis of ethnicity, thus obtaining ethnic cohesion. Still, it is important to note that they need not do so; disadvantaged people

may instead scramble for self-employment opportunities as isolated individuals. Therefore, in a strict sense, the hustling motivation imposed by labor force disadvantage is not ethnic in origin,
even though it does provide productive advantages to ethnic
firms.[26]

The lower-right square (table 2) describes nonethnic resources
that are nonproductive, including labor law evasion and tax cheat-
ing. Violations of wage, hour, and sanitary standards are endemic
in many small-business industries. Indeed, Lawrence Friedman
declares that the "modern welfare state has tended to criminalize
some small businesses, and squeeze others out of the market."[27]
For instance, regulatory sweeps of garment firms in Los Angeles
have recurrently found 90 percent or more in violation of labor
standards. Korean sewing contractors candidly acknowledged to
me that they must pay less than the statutory minimum wage in
order to get the contracts that keep them in business. Opportunities to violate wage, hour, and sanitary standards have also
attracted big corporate interests. That is, major corporations have
learned they can franchise a small-business entrepreneur who is
able to evade wage or sanitary laws with impunity, whereas the
parent corporation must comply. Since these evasions of law encourage small business, they constitute a covert, subterranean
resource of small-business firms. Naturally, ethnic and immigrant
firms share this unlawful and unproductive resource. But the
resource is not distinctively ethnic, and should not be confused
with resources derived from ethnicity.

### Policy Implications

Table 2 exposes several complexities of policy-making and policy implementation. The complexities arise because desirable and
undesirable conditions are jumbled together in ways difficult to
separate analytically—much less in administrative practice. On the
positive side, the productive ethnic resources identified in the
upper-left cell describe a reservoir of economic power that gener-
ates entrepreneurship and deserves public support. Public support means all public (and private philanthrophic) policies
intended to facilitate business growth by channeling public resources to growth nodules. Public resources include loans, gifts,

laws, exemptions, protections, and administrative attitudes that bear upon business growth.

Effective public support requires acknowledgment of the collective basis of entrepreneurship not only in the field of minority and ethnic business but in general public policies of small-business support. The alternative is policy based on "entrepreneurial individualism," the formation of public policy as though entrepreneurs were socially detached individualists. In most cases this assumption is factually wrong, and basing policy on it leads to misplacement of resources. Admittedly, entrepreneurs are sometimes socially detached individualists who, defying the odds, find economic success by being in just the right place at just the right time—for example, an individual who invested $5,000 in IBM in 1950 and never needed to work again. However, most entrepreneurs overcome the risks of business failure only by hard work, careful management, and effective utilization of resources peculiar to their situation. Therefore, public support should be based upon these realistic assumptions rather than on the faint possibility of getting rich quickly by means of a lucky strike.

Isolated individualists are as weak in business as in the rest of life. Their resources consist of a bank account, and, lacking concerned uncles, they cannot get a discount on anything they buy, so even their money does not go very far. By contrast, when entrepreneurs are linked to one another through mutually assisting networks (like ethnic groups), they can call upon collective resources, thus strengthening their genuinely productive capabilities. When public policies assume and select for support isolated individualists, the policies have selected people whose effective resources are just those actually bestowed upon them by public intervention. If they are loaned $10,000, that $10,000 is the effective limit of their resources. Public intervention has to provide the whole basis of their success, and because the cost of success is too high, the public resources allotted do not push a firm over the threshold of success. Hence, the whole investment is wasted. The best risks are those who, embedded in real social groups, have access to informal resources to supplement anything they may be granted by public policy. When public resources are allocated to such persons, the resources go farther; more entrepreneurs can be helped, and more can be accomplished with less effort.

Social embeddedness implies that entrepreneurs wish to change the world by means of their economic activity, and their strictly individual pecuniary interests are harmonious with this commitment. In contrast, the isolated individualist has only private economic motives. Since private hedonism does not create a value community, entrepreneurial individualists have to have a social goal in mind beyond self-enrichment in the world as it is now. As Andrew Carnegie once observed "The man who dies rich, dies disgraced." Carnegie's moral values linked him to a collectivity of like-minded persons sharing a vision of a desirable social order, and my claim is that social vision is not irrelevant to successful entrepreneurship. Public policy needs to find people who want to produce social change by means of economic activism. Their social goals need not be lofty. In the case of ethnic entrepreneurs, the welfare and good reputation of their ethnic group provide a social goal that often underscores individual economic activity. In any event, larger social goals cannot be cynically separated from entrepreneurship without weakening the entrepreneur's economic effectiveness. Therefore, social embeddedness is not a luxury that can be ignored by practical persons interested only in the profit statement. Finally, I would argue, minimal social embeddedness should be a desideratum of public policy, because anyone in business draws upon public resources of trust, order, and decency that he or she should be required to sustain, not just to exploit.

In the upper-right cell, table 2 identified resources that are productive but nonethnic. In my opinion, public policy should treat the class resources of immigrants (money and educational background) in tandem with and in supplementation to social embeddedness. That is, class resources being equal, that candidate's entrepreneurship is more promising who is socially embedded.

Labor force disadvantage becomes an entrepreneurial resource when it compels those afflicted to seek a living in self-employment. Obviously it should be no part of public policy to perpetuate labor force disadvantage in order to stimulate entrepreneurship. Indeed, most disadvantage results in such miserable entrepreneurship that it really represents a social problem concealed but not resolved through the medium of self-employment.[28] Thus, if immigrants hope to advance the welfare of their

ethnic group by means of economic activism, that is a laudable
motive. But it is unworthy to thrust this motive upon them by
discrimination in the labor market. In this sense, entrepreneurship should arise from positive vision rather than from
a social injustice, although much ethnic and religious entrepreneurship has arisen from negative roots, and the motive of
anger must be presumed to have appropriate cause and to be a
valid reason for entrepreneurship.

Restraint of trade, vertical integration, and organized crime
yield obvious potential for economic abuse, and are listed as
nonproductive (lower left) in table 2 for this reason. Nevertheless,
policymakers should not regard all of them as totally detrimental.
Solidarity, communication, and labor force disadvantage tend to
produce overcrowded, ethnically specialized, vertically integrated
small-business industries. As this situation is approached, coethnic
business owners develop both the motivation and the ability to
regulate internal competition in the interest of stable industrial
conditions. If the pottery industry is overcrowded with coethnics
(outsiders having been driven out), ethnic solidarity provides a
banner around which competitors can organize exclusive guilds,
even using racketeers to coerce recalcitrants. Ethnic integration,
then, can open some new opportunities for organized crime.

On the other hand, destructive competition is wasteful, and
vertical integration of ethnically dominated industries has some
justification in lower costs arising from efficiencies of communication. As Rein Peterson has observed, the Japanese make extensive
and effective use of officially regulated consortia among small
firms.[29] This is not true in Canada or the United States, where
governments do nothing to strengthen small firms through cooperative arrangements and, instead, assume that industrial cooperation takes place only at the expense of the consumer. This
simple-minded policy might be reexamined to ascertain whether,
excluding the obviously negative cases, there is in fact some possibility of effecting productive improvements in small-business
industries by encouraging or, at least, tolerating cooperation.

Indeed, as we turn to the final square of table 2, we can see how
integration may help to cancel some of the nonproductive activities listed there, for guilds commonly take a positive role in
restraining the violations of law that competition makes endemic
in immigrant-populated industries. Business crimes probably in-

crease when, under conditions of hypercompetition, business returns sink below the survival minimum. As a result, firms must ignore wage, sanitary, and labor laws that impose costs upon their products or services.

In California, for example, law enforcement task forces have swept through the garment industry in repeated drives to apprehend and punish violators of labor law and to force the garment industry to comply with existing labor and sanitary legislation. In the past, racketeers performed the same service on a profit-making basis, breaking the legs and bombing the business premises of those who resisted the industrial standard. In fact, the law enforcement chief of the garment task force in Los Angeles wryly remarked that his role was, and was understood to be, analogous to that played by racketeers in the garment industry of yore.

In the competitive, ethnically pluralistic garment industry of Los Angeles, state task forces have been the only counterpressure tending to bring this crime-riddled industry into compliance with existing labor legislation. However, as coethnic guilds form, they acquire both the motive and the ability to take over some of the regulatory function, relieving the state of the burden and tending to restore minimal standards to low-wage industries. We found Korean, Chinese, and Latin American sewing contractors' associations in the Los Angeles garment industry, although none was yet powerful enough to impose standards upon the industry. If in the long run the ethnic contractors' associations should acquire more market power, they would acquire the ability to impose upgraded labor conditions, thus tending to restore law and order to their industry more effectively than do law enforcement sweeps. For this reason policy-making authorities should encourage the gradual formation of ethnic guilds.

Tax evasion represents an almost identical situation. Social security taxes are often ignored by small employers, especially those whose labor force is largely illegal, and income taxes are also underpaid by small-business owners who represent, in the opinion of the Internal Revenue Service, one of the most noncompliant occupations. Testifying before the Joint Economic Committee of the U.S. Congress, Peter Guttman declared that the subterranean economy is "very important" to the welfare of small business.

Small business is prominent in those areas of the economy where cash receipts are a substantial portion of tax receipts. Small business effectively receives a subsidy, not as a matter of law, but as a matter of practice, through the substantial amount of cash income which escapes the tax collector.[30]

Naturally, income tax evasion in small business will not end until the IRS develops aggressive, new procedures for collection and enforcement, but if coethnic guilds obtain regulatory control over competitive industries, they are in a position to reduce the hyper-competitive conditions that encourage tax evasion. As a matter of fact, it becomes a vested industrial interest of a regulatory guild to produce enough tax compliance in its industry to prevent IRS audits. Therefore, given the rampant disregard of tax and labor law now prevailing in hypercompetitive, small-business industries, a dose of ethnic collectivism might be in the public interest.

## Conclusion

Ethnic entrepreneurship bears some resemblance to a social movement, and policies based upon the assumption of entrepreneurial individualism fail as a result. Rather, polices should acknowledge the social dimension of entrepreneurship in order to increase their effectiveness. Fear of monopolistic abuse of market position has some basis in reality, but is exaggerated and imbalanced, for law enforcement capability also increases as immigrant ethnics acquire market power. On balance, the social benefits of labor and tax code enforcement are likely to outweigh costs to consumers arising from the formation of cartels.

## Notes

1. Frank H. Knight, *Risk, Uncertainty, and Profit* (Boston and New York, 1921), 278–300; Armen A. Alchian and Harold Demsetz, "Production, Information Costs, and Economic Organization," *American Economic Review* (1972): 777–95.

2. Knight, 300; William J. Baumol, "Entrepreneurship in Economic Theory," *American Economic Review* 58 (1968): 64-71

3. Knight, 283.

4. Joseph Schumpeter, *The theory of Economic Development*, trans. Redvers Opie (Cambridge, 1934), 81. See also Andrew A. Beveridge and Anthony R.

Oberschall, *African Businessmen and Development in Zambia* (Princeton, 1971), 284–86.

5. Peter Kilby, "Hunting the Heffalump," in Peter Kilby, ed., *Entrepreneurship and Economic Development* (New York, 1971), 3–6.

6. Frank W. Young, "A Macrosociological Interpretation of Entrepreneurship," in Kilby, *Entrepreneurship*, 140.

7. David McClelland with David Winter, *Motivating Economic Achievement* (New York, 1971), 6.

8. Arthur Francis, "Families, Firms, and Finance Capital: The Development of UK Industrial Firms With Particular Reference to Their Ownership and Control," *Sociology* 14 (1980): 2. See also T. S. Ashton, *The Industrial Revolution, 1760–1830* (London, 1948), 19.

9. Max Weber, *The Protestant Ethic and the Spirit of Capitalism*, trans. Talcott Parsons, 2d ed. (New York, 1958); David McClelland, "The Achievement Motive in Economic Growth," in Kilby, *Entrepreneurship*, 109–22; George A. DeVos, *Socialization for Achievement* (Berkeley and Los Angeles, 1973), 2:562–82.

10. Young, 140–42.

11. Ibid., 140.

12. Nathaniel Leff, "Industrial Organization and Entrepreneurship in the Developing Countries: The Economic Groups," *Economic Development and Cultural Change* 26 (1978): 664.

13. Marlene Sway, "Gypsies as a Middleman Minority," (Ph.D. diss. UCLA, 1983); Leroy Jones and Il Sakong, *Government, Business and Entrepreneurship in Economic Development: The Korean Case* (Cambridge, 1980).

14. R. A. Schermerhorn, "Jews without Middleman Status: Their Historic Position in China and India," *Journal of Intercultural Studies* 2 (1981): 19; Beveridge and Oberschall, 285.

15. Marlys Harris, "How the Koreans Won the Greengrocer Wars," *Money* 12 (1983): 190–98.

16. Kilby, in Kilby, *Entrepreneurs*, 27–28.

17. Ivan Light, *Ethnic Enterprise in America: Business and Welfare Among Chinese, Japanese and Blacks* (Berkeley and Los Angeles, 1972).

18. Robert Jarvenpa and Walter P. Zenner, "Scots in the Northern Fur Trade: A Middleman Minority Perspective," paper presented at the annual meeting of the Anthropological Association (Los Angeles, 16 November 1978).

19. Leff, 671.

20. Roland I. Robinson, "The Financing of Small Business in the United States," in Stuart W. Bruchey, ed., *Small Business in American Life* (New York, 1980), 280.

21. Abner Cohen, "Cultural Strategies in the Organization of Trading Diasporas," in Claude Meillassoux, ed., *The Development of Indigenous Trade and Markets in West Africa* (London, 1971), 267.

22. Ibid., 271.

23. Light, *Ethnic Enterprise*, 94–98.

24. Ivan Light, "Immigrant and Ethnic Enterprise in North America," *Ethnic and Racial Studies* 7 (1984): 195–216.

25. Knight, 352.

26. Ivan Light, *Cities in World Perspective* (New York, 1983), 372–73.

27. Lawrence M. Friedman, "Law and Small Business in the United States: One Hundred Years of Struggle and Accommodation," in Bruchey, *Small Business*, 315.

28. Joseph S. Chung, "Small Ethnic Business as a Form of Disguised Unemployment and Cheap Labor," U.S. Commission on Civil Rights, *Civil Rights Issues of Asian and Pacific Americans* (Washington, 1979), 509–17.

29. Rein Peterson, *Small Business: Building a Balanced Economy* (Erin, Ontario, 1977), 150.

30. Joint Economic Committee, The Underground Economy, 96th Congress, 1st. sess., 1980, 26–27.

# "Ethnicity and Business Enterprise": A Comment

RANDALL M. MILLER

It should really be no surprise to learn that business, especially small business, performs more than economic functions. Indeed, the very existence of small business, and of ethnic enterprise, provides symbolic proof that the American Dream retains its vitality. The proliferation of independent economic units, of numerous self-employed, supposedly economically independent people, promises to preserve political democracy and ensure social stability—or so assumes traditional republican political economy. Small businesses, and ethnic enterprise in that setting, have provided folk heroes of the American way. In a republic founded on the civic virtue of the self-reliant citizen, the entrepreneur represents the guardian of republican ideology and order.[1]

Even immigrants have accepted this basic definition of the American ideal, suggesting the powerful, if subtle unspoken, ideological imperatives that may have been at work to nudge so many different immigrants into small business, even as small business seemed to become more precarious and outdated in the modern industrial age. It is the lure of entrepreneurship that provides the occasion for the discussion of ethnicity and business enterprise, for the functions and effects of ethnic enterprise derive from the motives of those who followed their various American dreams. In assessing the interplay between ethnicity and entrepreneurship, however, we must not grow nostalgic about our folk heroes or the purity of our forebears' desires.

Social values, customs, and public policy, among many other noneconomic factors, all influence the forms and performances of business organizations. Businessmen perceive such factors through social and cultural lenses, of course, for each businessman lives in the society in which his business operates. Ivan Light appreciates all of this in his arguments about social embeddedness, and he offers a suggestive case for a policy that will sustain ethnic entrepreneurship in the modern age.

In essence, Light maintains a dialectical perspective. He agrees with Edna Bonacich and John Modell that ethnicity supports the ethnic economy and, in turn, the ethnic economy perpetuates ethnicity.[2] Ethnicity creates hostility toward the ethnic group, which must fall back on its indigenous resources in order to survive, thereby reinforcing ethnicity and exacerbating hostility and so on, according to the Bonacich-Modell argument. Ethnic enterprise emerges from such a dialectic, at first drawing upon the group's cultural and economic resources, but later, through its profitability, contributing to ethnic solidarity and counteracting the forces of assimilation—public education, mass media, the marketplace, or whatever. In his multivariate approach to ethnic enterprise, Light makes a strong case for an interplay of class and culture in ethnic economic behavior, but in the end he identifies cultural forces as the key determinants.

Some problems intrude to weaken such arguments. Light's and Bonacich and Modell's preoccupation with California settings and Asian immigrants skews the evidence somewhat. One wonders how Dominicans in Jersey City, New Jersey, or Haitians in Miami, Florida, might fit Light's model. Even Light's limited focus on Koreans might be extended profitably to compare the adaptation of the Koreans coming to America in the 1970s and 1980s, many of whom are well-educated, urban, and middle-class people, with the experiences of the earlier Korean arrivals, most of whom were poor and rural folk. In a recent book, Illsoo Kim suggests that the Korean immigrants of the 1970s in New York have developed a unique "community" by forming geographically dispersed, segmented voluntary associations rather than relying on territorial concentration, as have Koreans in Los Angeles.[3]

Self-employment might also reflect something besides ethnicity at work. For instance, there has been a recent general upswing in self-employment across America because of the shift from an industrial to a service economy, and ethnic enterprise has no doubt benefited from the trend. In fact, changing life-styles have also encouraged many middle-class Americans, including WASPs, to leave the city for the countryside to set up craft shops and other small businesses or to move into gentrified city districts to open restaurants and stores.

Light's emphasis on retailers, manufacturers, and their cooperative associations also neglects the family economy generally and such individualistic activities as real estate investment, one of the most important means of capital accumulation among ethnic entrepreneurs. Crime, too, bears investigation as a small-business enterprise in its own right. Moreoever, by focusing on ethnic businessmen who used ethnic community connections to achieve some degree of collectivism, Light ignores those immigrant and minority entrepreneurs who never joined such organizations but instead distrusted them. Can they all be dismissed as "socially-detached individualists," or hedonists even?

- On the last point, it is necessary to get down to cases. The road from some brand of collectivist behavior to flat-out capitalism is uneven. It varies not only among ethnic groups, but within each one. Factors such as location, personality, leadership, and luck, to name several, all influence the rate and nature of shifts from one form of economic behavior and concern to another.

Even terminology is elusive. How does one measure "success" when the very idea of American business success might be rooted in myth? Thomas Cochran, in *200 Years of American Business*, reminds us that Americans have fallen victim to a false ethos of confidence about the supposed superiority of American business practices, equating the *size* of American economic growth with genius in management and business organization.[4] The low *rate* of American economic growth since World War II has shaken that confidence somewhat, but it has also called into question all traditional measurements of successful business practices in America. So, too, has Japanese penetration of American markets.

For some ethnic groups, success has never been counted in material terms. But even among "highly successful" ethnic groups in America, especially the Jews who rank close to the top in "making it in America," high income or wealth is not the sole spur. Although many Jews have sought places in law and medicine, for example, their tendency to engage in medical research or civil rights cases—the least lucrative areas within those professions—suggests that traditional definitions of success might not apply. Familial bonds and service to God and the community, for many groups, determine a man's worth. Ask any good Catholic brought up under the Baltimore Catechism.

If, for the purpose of argument, however, we accept the assumption that economic advance is the basic goal of entrepreneurship, does it follow that all individuals, all groups, will seek the same degree or rate of advance? How, even when, do we measure success or failure when dealing with business activity? Nevertheless, these and other questions should not detract from Light's principal purpose or his significant achievement in mastering the large literature on ethnic enterprise—a field teeming with academic entrepreneurs.

Light's conclusions require application. He argues that because class and cultural resources are unequally distributed and developed among otherwise equally disadvantaged ethnic groups, various peoples evince unequal rates of entrepreneurship. Groups with more resources outperform groups with less. The implications of such unequal rates of entrepreneurship are important to consider, for in this issue we find the entree to racism, social change, and the American character.

To put the question another way, why have some groups prospered and others languished in America? If bigotry contributes to a group's entrepreneurship, as Light and others imply, why have blacks and Hispanics not done at least as well as Asians and Jews? This is a politically charged question. Most people think they know why some have made it and others have not. It is because people are different; they respond differently to the same social and economic stimuli. George Washington Plunkitt of Tammany Hall once preached the American Dream in what he hoped would be his epitaph: "I seen my opportunities and I took 'em." But one man's chance is another man's danger.

In explaining people's varying responses to similar circumstances or forces, scholars offer no consensus and rarely maintain any single explanation in raw form. But one of the most conventional arguments about ethnic success in business posits racism or discrimination as the main reason why some groups lag behind in the way to wealth; that is, those groups have not had equal access to opportunity. Another argument suggests that class retards or promotes economic advance, that one's position in the socio economic structure determines what opportunities will be available, as well as what resources and what degree of recognition will be at hand to encourage action on those opportunities. Both explanations cast some blame on society for inhibiting the economic rise of lower-class and racially oppressed groups and, in the end, insist that government correct inequities in the marketplace, for the groups cannot help themselves alone.

A third explanation places responsibility for success or failure within the groups themselves. The high visibility of the Japanese and Jews among American "achievers" suggests, on the face of it, that racism or prejudice and even class, perhaps, do not necessarily prevent economic progress. Neither group received any direct assistance from government, and the Japanese were once divested of their property by governmental policies, yet both groups got ahead anyway. Thus their achievement further suggests that external support is not necessary. According to this view, the cultural predispositions of some groups push them ahead in the American economic stream, while others, for similar reasons, flounder.

In still another interpretation, Stephen Steinberg, in *The Ethnic Myth,* measures success in terms of income rather than entrepreneurship and contends that historical timing and position, more than culture, have determined the economic success of white ethnics and the comparable failure of blacks. The former entered an expanding labor market while the latter remained locked in rural poverty. By the time blacks moved northward to share in the fruits of industrial and business growth, the rapidly changing economy no longer demanded many unskilled workers. Then, racism prevented blacks from acquiring the technical skills necessary to compete with the children of the immigrants in a post industrial society.[5]

Stanley Lieberson offers a more convincing variation on that same theme by observing that immigrants were always in a better position to adapt to changes in the American economy because they could move freely, coming to the United States and migrating about to capitalize on opportunities or departing when no such opportunities arose. Blacks, by contrast, were never so free to move, having been forcibly brought to America and shackled by law and customs as slaves and as freedmen to a poor agricultural, region.[6] Today's heightened movement of blacks between North and South intimates a pattern of free movement that may, in part, explain the improvements in many blacks' economic positions after World War II.

Light, among others, illustrates the importance of timing and positioning very well.[7] He argues that trust among fellow ethnic group members forges the vital component in building successful ethnic enterprises. He might add that it also aids immeasurably in sustaining them. Asian growers of Oriental vegetables in southern New Jersey, for example, enjoy a competitive advantage over their non-Asian rivals for the Philadelphia market because the wholesalers and retail grocers who purchase most of the vegetables are also Asians who prefer to deal with their own people.[8]

The ability of entrepreneurs to raise money to begin businesses and to borrow small sums of money to keep them going often derives from family sources, but it also comes from community trust, nurtured in the benevolent associations, mutual aid societies, churches, and other organizations that spring up to promote collective responses to new socio economic conditions. Thus an institutional arrangement exists among many ethnic groups to facilitate small-business activity. Supposedly, the absence of such an arrangement militates against the development of small-business sectors. Perhaps, too, institutional ties not only provide the climate of mutual assistance conducive to modest capital recruitment and risk-taking but also develop a business sense among the organizations' leaders so that they serve as managerial guides as well as sources of capital and support. One wonders here why blacks have not fared better. Historically, blacks have had a semblance of sustainable institutional frameworks with their churches, freedmen's banks and savings clubs, and fraternal societies, and they even have had a history of successful small-business activity going back to the colonial era. Perhaps, then, something more than collective trust is necessary, something more than geographical concentration or local support, to make it in America.

John Modell in his study of Japanese economic adaptation in America offers a twist on Light's theme that might prove instructive. He states that Japanese entrepreneurship in agriculture and commerce was a response to prejudice and discrimination and that solidarity was a consequence of Japanese concentration in particular occupations rather than a cause of their success.[9] This conclusion, however, does not stress cultural predispositions toward small-business activity but points to positioning. And it does not really answer the question, again, of why the Japanese have made it and others, say blacks, have not. In any case, when external pressures weakened after World War II, the second generation of Japanese began to enter the professions rather than continue with the old family businesses, thereby eroding ethnic solidarity and with it the ability to sustain the ethnic enterprises on the old terms. Ethnic businesses might survive only so long as ethnic enclaves persist, for such firms seem to function best in ethnic "free enterprise zones," insulated in particular services and products from national competitors.

One wonders, moreover, whether ethnic small business is always good for a community. Much of the capital earned in such enterprises has been plowed back into the businesses or has gone to educating the sons of the entrepreneurs. Such personal capital accumulation in the form of education does not always redound to the small businesses' advantage. College or professional training, for example, might improve the family business only by sacrificing the very qualities that gave it meaning and its modest success—the practices of extended credit, collectivism, intensive family labor and service to a very specialized, insulated market. Furthermore, ethnic small business has not always been a source of neighborhood economic development. Economic growth does not come from businesses with few employees who are paid low wages and who must submit to the arbitrary rule of employers. With any improvement in the quality of the labor pool or conditions of work the small business must assume new, perhaps prohibitive, costs in social as well as dollar terms. How, for example, will the employer with only a grade school education interact with employees who have high school diplomas or with his own children who have college degrees?

How, too, will ethnically intensive businesses survive in changing local markets when they discriminate against "outsiders"? One example will make the point. A recent correspondent to *TIME* magazine, reacting to a feature story on Los Angeles's new immigrants, related that she could not get her check cashed at her local Korean-owned grocery, despite working, living, and shopping in the same neighborhood for twenty years.[10] The Korean entrepreneur's policy was that only fellow Koreans had any credit or check-cashing privileges. Ethnic neighborhoods do not remain static even when inhabited by people of the same national background. As neighborhood populations change, new social dynamics and economic pressures will enter the workplace and the marketplace to recast the activities of ethnic small businesses, or those businesses will not be likely to survive.

A related question is the place of public involvement in the

formation and development of any small business. In treating
ethnic enterprise, Light is one of the few writers willing to explore
the effects of regulation on business character and behavior. Small
businesses cannot easily bear the costs of regulations—minimum
wages, safety precautions, worker compensation, open hiring, or
even the paperwork involved. Unless they assume such burdens,
however, they remain limited in their ability to enter the larger
national market. With urban decay, internal or local growth will
not suffice to keep the old businesses profitable, to satisfy the
owners' children's higher expectations of material rewards, and to
hold the ethnic collectives intact. As Stuart Butler shows in his
book, *Enterprise Zones,* regulation and taxation, in the 1960s and
1970s especially, have reduced the birthrate of new businesses and
crippled or killed older ones in many urban districts, so that even
the supposed advantages of low-cost labor no longer compen-
sate.[11]

On the local level, small shopkeepers and tradesmen have generally been able to protect their competitive positions, often by
ignoring governmental regulations, but on the federal level they
have met defeat. Ethnic small-business owners exert no influence
in Washingotn, all the political rhetoric about creating jobs in
cities notwithstanding. They do not even form an identifiable
interest group in the broker politics of America. Nobody really
speaks for the needs of the family-run small business in an ethnic
enclave. Federal laws and regulations respond to other interests
and, too often, threaten small enterprises. Urban renewal is an
obvious example. If, as Lawrence Friedman asserts in an excellent
review of law and small business in America, the law plays a
configurative role in defining the boundaries of business activity
without necessarily determining specific business practices, small-
businessowners without a voice in Washington or much of a collective voice anywhere can survive only by "finding niches and cre-
vices in the market."[12] Ethnic small businesses do just that, but
necessarily they remain small and insecure. Ethnicity might be a
means of locating interstitial opportunities and exploiting them,
but it will provide only limited opportunities in an economy and
society undergoing significant and rapid change.

No doubt ethnic enterprise will not go away. Small businesses
still contitute more than 90 percent of all business enterprises in
the United States, and although multinational companies domi-

nate the marketplace, small businesses, including ethnic ones, play important roles in services, retailing, and production of specialized products. But the character of small business will change to meet new market realities, for, in the end, small businesses of all kinds exist to make money, and making money requires at least some adaptation to market conditions. The Korean grocer in the story related above will have to accept checks from non-Koreans and new Korean immigrants if he wants to keep their trade. In big business, questions of management loom large in explanations of success or failure, but in small business, success or failure often turns on such factors as alertness to new technology and the cultivation of highly specialized markets. Small businesses must take risks if they are going to succeed, and success in traditional terms usually involves growth. The small business either becomes an adjunct of a big company providing supply or distribution services or, by building on somne new product or innovation to attract substantial capital, becomes big itself. Either way, the small businesses lose many of their primordial entrepreneurial and cultural peculiarities. It is this process of change in response to market conditions that now begs ethnic scholarship. What happens to the second and third generations of ethnic businesses, and how much of what happens to them is a product of external factors—government, economy, technology, education, and social structure—and how much is a result of the more elusive, but no less powerful and real, internal or cultural forces we have learned about today?

## Notes

1. Rowland Berthoff, "Independence and Enterprise: Small Business in the American Dream," in Stuart W. Bruchey, ed., *Small Business in American Life* (New York, 1980), 28–48.

2. Edna Bonachich and John Modell, *The Economic Basis of Ethnic Solidarity: Small Business in the Japanese American Community* (Berkeley and Los Angeles, 1980).

3. Illsoo Kim, *New Urban Immigrants: The Korean Community in New York* (Princeton, 1981).

4. Thomas Cochran, *200 Years of American Business* (New York, 1977), xiii–xiv and passim.

5. Stephen Steinberg, *The Ethnic Myth: Race, Ethnicity, and Class in America* (New York, 1981), especially 173–200.

6. Stanley Lieberson, *A Piece of the Pie: Blacks and White Immigrants Since 1880* (Berkeley and Los Angeles, 1980), 36–37 and passim.

7. See, especially, Ivan Light, *Ethnic Enterprise in America: Business and Welfare among Chinese, Japanese and Blacks* (Berkeley and Los Angeles, 1972); John Modell, *The Economics and Politics of Racial Accommodation: The Japanese of Los Angeles, 1900–1942* (Urbana, Ill., 1977); and Bonacich and Modell. For some varying views, see the essays in Scott Cummings, ed., *Self-Help in Urban America: Patterns of Minority Business Enterprise* (Port Washington, N.Y., 1980).

8. Marc Duvoisin, "Asian Farmers Meeting an American Demand," *The Philadelphia Inquirer,* 29 August 1983.

9. Modell, *Economics and Politics of Racial Accommodation.*

10. Edith Broughton (Glendale, California) to Editors, *Time* 122 (1 August 1983): 6.

11. Stuart M. Butler, *Enterprise Zones: Greenlining the Inner Cities* (New York, 1981).

12. Lawrence Friedman, "Law and Small Business in the United States: One Hundred Years of Struggle and Accommodation," in Bruchey, *Small Business in American Life,* 315.

# "Ethnicity and Business Enterprise": A Comment

## Kenneth L. Kusmer

Although almost all studies of ethnic or minority group behavior deal to some extent with entrepreneurial activity, relatively few take business enterprise as the central focus. Ivan Light has attempted to provide us with a comprehensive overview of the shifting pattern of entrepreneurialism among minority groups, and to accomplish this task he has surveyed an extensive sociological literature on the subject. He finds that the level and success of business activity for any specific ethnic group is related to both ethnic resources and class resources, that some element of both is always evident, but that the "mix" of these two factors varies greatly depending upon the group's cultural values as well as upon the skills and monetary resources at its disposal. Nevertheless, Light believes there has been a general shift from ethnicity to class over the twentieth century, and not surprisingly, he finds that blacks represent a rather extreme case within this general model. As he stated over a decade ago in his book *Ethnic Enterprise in America,* Light argues that blacks have often been lacking in both class *and* ethnic resources. One result is that they have been unable to utilize rotating credit associations based upon kinship ties, as some Asian groups did so successfully.[1] Oddly, however, Light then contends that, contrary to popular assumption, blacks are not totally devoid of the entrepreneurial spirit. In fact, there is probably "much higher than average self-employment among economically marginal blacks" because researchers fail to take into account the large number of urban Negroes who engage in the combination of legal, semilegal, and illegal activities known in the ghetto as "hustling."

Although one could criticize a number of specific points that Light makes, I think it is more useful to place these in the wider

43

context of a more general critique. As a theoretical overview, the essay has considerable value, and the fundamental shift from ethnicity toward class-based activities and resources provides a useful model that can give us considerable insight into the development of ethnic enterprise in North America. Yet despite its seeming breadth, this perspective is inadequate in several respects.

First and foremost, there is simply not enough historical context to Light's generalizations. Not a single source on black urban history is consulted, not even the classic sociological study by St. Clair Drake and Horace Cayton, *Black Metropolis,* which is a very good source of information on black business in Chicago in the 1920s and 1930s.[2] Even for white ethnic groups, however, well-known historical studies have not been utilized. From Oscar Handlin's *Boston's Immigrants* to Kathleen Neils Conzen's study of antebellum Milwaukee to Theodore Hershberg's edited volume on Philadelphia social history, there are numerous historical works that not only can give us added insight into the development of entrepreneurial activity among minority groups, but also can make the abstractions of theory more meaningful in human terms.[3]

In additiion to a stronger and more exact sense of historical development than sociological theory can present, there is a need to place ethnic entrepreneurs in a *community context.* This cannot be emphasized too much. In describing "collective" styles of entrepreneurship used by Asian immigrants, Light briefly mentions the value of "ethnic community networks." But we need to be more attentive to a larger sense of the significance of the ethnic community, in which entrepreneurs were related to a geographic place, to ethnic institutions, and to kinship networks whose function often superseded the profit motive. It is the ethnic entrepreneur's relationship to the community of which he is a member, not merely to his fellow entrepreneurs, that is important. Fundamentally, I believe that a historically grounded, community-centered approach to ethnic enterprise provides a valuable alternative to the strictly sociological perspective on this phenomenon, although ideally an integration of these two approaches would be most persuasive.

A community-centered approach to ethnic enterprise parallels, to some extent, the critique of the literature on social mobility that historian James Henretta has recently propounded. Henretta has stressed the need to understand the cultural values of minority and working-class groups in their own terms instead of imposing on their behavior possibly false frameworks, drawn from twentieth-century middle-class life-styles. Upward mobility in a careerist sense was not necessarily a concern (and, in many cases, not a possibility realistically) of immigrant working-class people in the nineteenth century.[4] I would argue that a similar approach has to be taken when studying the history of entrepreneurial activity among ethnic groups.

In the nineteenth century, especially, there was a symbiotic relationship between the ethnic working class and the more successful members of the community. Upward mobility occurred for ethnic businessmen, but within a context of reciprocal community obligations that contained the upwardly mobile, as Conzen has pointed out concerning the German community of nineteenth-century Milwaukee.[5] Likewise, Victor Greene, commenting on the social functions of Polish saloon keepers, gives us an understanding of the communal significance of entrepreneurs in ethnic neighborhoods generally. The proprietors "provided necessary services such as holding the immigrants' earnings—the so-called 'immigrant banks'—notarizing papers, forwarding money orders home, acting as transportation agents, affording accommodations, interpreting and translating, giving generous credit to countrymen, and even writing letters for the illiterate. Their business hours were convenient, and the interested parties conducted negotiations over lager." Much the same could be said of Slovak grocers and saloonkeepers.[6] Even the Italian *padrone,* who clearly took advantage of his charges for his own financial benefit, performed useful social as well as economic functions for immigrants and helped ease their adjustment to life in a new and sometimes hostile environment.[7]

This is not to say that no class divisions arose within ethnic communities. There was always the potential for that, especially when (as happened in a number of instances) the entrepreneurs of an immigrant community came from a different region of Europe than the bulk of the working class. Disproportionate numbers of German Jews, German-born Poles, and northern Italians assumed middle-class roles in their respective communities.[8] The potential for deep community and class divisions was especially great in the Jewish communities of eastern cities, where German Jews had arrived up to two generations before their Russian coreligionists and had often assimilated Anglo-Saxon norms and had risen in economic and social status to a remarkable degree. Yet an overarching sense of communal solidarity was gradually forged by the common threat of a growing anti-Semitism and by a recognition of the bonds of a religious tradition that spanned differences between Reform Judaism and Orthodoxy.[9]

In his recent study of ethnicity and industrialization in Detroit, Olivier Zunz shows the many connections that existed between ethnic entrepreneurs and the communities in which they resided. Especially for the larger groups (Germans and Irish), a degree of upward mobility was possible within the community. "In 1880, a German blacksmith could have developed a small carriage factory in the German neighborhood and grown modestly prosperous within this group of origin."[10] By the turn of the century, however, ethnic entrepreneurs had to relate to two competing social and economic systems. One led outward, to a new, emerging bureaucratic world of corporate-dominated industry, where the ladder of success would be through the managerial system.[11] The other was the traditional community base. It is significant that in 1900 in Detroit the three largest companies owned by German immigrants on the traditionally German east side of the city were producing goods that were marginal to the main thrust of industrial America at that time: They consisted of a brewery, a spectacle factory, and a furniture company. More successful than the proprietors of those businesses, in purely monetary terms, was the second-generation German Frank Hecker, the president of American Car and Foundry. Hecker built a French Renaissance-style mansion in a predominantly Anglo-Saxon elite area, joined exclusive clubs, and was completely accepted among the new industrial leaders who were transforming the city's—and the nation's—economy.[12]

In 1900 the community roots of many ethnic businessmen still remained strong. Nevertheless, twenty years later class-oriented social divisions were nearly complete for the older immigrant groups, and they tended now to separate themselves out more by social class than by ethnic identity. "The German community, which was still a cross-class community in the 1890s, economically based on independent small enterprises, disappeared under the pressures of industrialization and of the ideological trauma associated with the First World War."[13]

In 1920 the new immigrant groups from Southern and Eastern Europe were highly segregated, but not in the manner of earlier immigrants of the nineteenth century. Hungarian and Polish factory operatives now took over large parts of the city near the big plants. "In the process, the Polish neighborhood of the 1890s, with its atmosphere of a compact village, its isolated institutional and social life . . . and its ability to retain the more successful Poles as shopkeepers or professionals, had given way to the classic mill-town of workers, retaining not most but only a handful of non-workers within its ranks."[14] In Detroit, only the small community of Russian Jews retained the nineteenth-century tradition of occupational diversity in 1920, the terminal date of Zunz's analysis. In Cleveland, in many ways a similar city, it is evident that by 1930 the Russian Jewish community was beginning to undergo the same fragmentation along ethno-class lines that other groups had already experienced. This was also true of that city's Italian population, which had been amazingly compact prior to World War I. By 1930 the Italian middle class and elite had largely moved out to new suburban enclaves. Still to some extent segregated by ethnicity, they were no longer part of a consolidated geographic entity.[15] The ethnic entrepreneurs' ties of solidarity to their group were weakened by this transformation but not obliterated so easily as some modernization theorists would have us believe. Many ethnic enterprises earn large returns of their investments, but there is a continuing paradox in this fact because ethnic businessmen do not necessarily put profit above the needs of kin and community.

During the era of nascent industrialization, black businessmen were in an entirely different situation from their white ethnic counterparts. In the late nineteenth century, the most successful black businessmen served a predominantly white clientele (for example, caterers, barbershop proprietors who served whites, and retail dealers who were centrally located). Furthermore, many of these entrepreneurs lived in integrated areas away from the main areas of black settlement. So these individuals, unlike white ethnic entrepreneurs, were not community-based. The fate of these black businessmen was tragic. The growth of the black ghetto on the one hand and increasing racism among whites on the other undercut their businesses. Beginning in the 1890s, they were gradually superseded by a new black elite composed of ghetto-based retail dealers and an increasing number of black profession-als who also served a black clientele.[16] But the new black busi-nesses suffered grievously because as consumers blacks had little to spend on anything beyond basic necessities and because, unlike white ethnics, black entrepreneurs were unable to rely very much upon the family economy to pool capital. As a result of disease, malnutrition, and high infant mortality rates there was a paucity of teenaged children in many black families during this period.[17] In addition, of course, black entrepreneurs suffered discrimina-tion from white lending institututions, which made it hard for them to expand operations.

Black failure in the business realm was due fundamentally to these outside forces—not to any cultural incapacity for en-trepreneurship. One proof of this is the brief upsurge of black business activity that occurred when blacks began to make some modest economic gains after World War I. For the first time, blacks living in cities were able to obtain industrial employment—even though in most cases these jobs were of an unskilled nature. Despite the high rents that many blacks had to pay at this time, steady wages among the Afro-American working class yielded an increase in entrepreneurial efforts. In Cleveland, for example, the relative index of blacks owning retail stores increased from 18 in 1910 to 29 in 1930. This was still far below parity (represented by 100), but it was a measurable increase nonetheless. And the comparable figure for blacks owning restaurants or lunchrooms was much higher, reaching an index of 81 in 1930. These busi-nesses were quite small, of course, but then so was the amount of capital at their owners' disposal.[18] Unfortunately, the Great De-pression dealt a death blow to many black enterprises that had been expanding before 1929. In Cleveland, the businesses estab-lished by leading black entrepreneur Herbert Chauncey (who set up the city's first black bank and also was involved in real estate and insurance) collapsed during the early 1930s, and the fall of the legendary Jesse Binga in Chicago occurred at the same time.[19]

Sociologists and economists usually use legitimate business firms as a measure of entrepreneurial activity, but in a com-munity-centered approach to ethnic enterprise, a broader defini-tion is required. Certainly, illegal enterprises also must be

considered. Much more important than "hustling" has been organized crime. Gambling, prostitution, bootlegging, policy games,
and so on have played a significant role in the history of ethnic
America, as Irish, Jewish, and Italian criminals dominated various
aspects of organized crime long before blacks did. Still, because of
the relative poverty of blacks and their exclusion from many types
of legitimate employment, illegal activities probably did play a
greater economic role in the black community at an earlier stage.
As Drake and Cayton have indicated, the policy racket was a very
important "business" on the South Side of Chicago in the 1920s
and 1930s—one not affected at all by the Great Depression. For
white ethnics as well as blacks, the attitude toward organized-
crime figures was often ambivalent. This was not simply because
such individuals were symbols of success through illegitimate
means, but also because, like their legitimate counterparts, they
often made their "personal" profit rebound to the benefit of their
respective communities—through jobs provided and philanthropy extended. As Jenna Weissman Joselit points out in her
study of Jewish crime in New York in the early twentieth century,
ethnic criminals even provided a regulatory function in some
industries. "By fixing prices and providing steady jobs, racketeers
stabilized the volatile garment industry; Jewish poultry racketeers
did much the same thing. They too regulated competition, fixed
prices, provided jobs for poultry workmen, and thus steadied
what was inherently an unsteady business."[20] In some ways, the
symbiotic relationship between organized crime figures and their
ethnic communities has been more signficant than that evidenced
by legitimate businessmen.

A community-based perspective on ethnic entrepreneurialism
should also consider the importance of sports or entertainment
figures and their promoters, individuals whose occupations often
overlapped or were intertwined with the underworld of crime.[21]
It is probable that among blacks especially, entertainment has
been significant historically as an outlet for entrepreneurial tend-
encies stifled by discrimination in other areas of endeavor. Black
theaters began to fail in the 1920s as a result of the high cost of
producing and attending theatrical engagements; competition
from movie houses also hurt the black legitimate stage.[22] But the
world of music was different. One needed very little capital to set
up a band, and the cabarets and nightclubs that blossomed in the

post-World War I era provided plenty of employment for the
jazzman and the blues singer. This was true not only for major
centers of black music such as Harlem and Chicago, but of most of
the urban areas to which blacks migrated after 1916. Occupational
statistics for northern cities show that, proportionately, there were
at least two to three times as many black musicians as there were
whites in the music business at that time. The increase in black
musicians was partly a response to the needs of more culturally
conscious black audiences in the cities. Black entertainers also
benefited, however, from the increased patronage of whites, who
began to flock to black entertainment spots in the 1920s.[23]

Finally, a thorough history of ethnic enterprise must take a
careful look at the world of urban politics. Here again, a broad
definition of entrepreneurialism is necessary. For American ethnic groups there has often been a close relationship between
politics and business; the distinction between the two has not
always been clear-cut, and both have operated in a community
context that has given a broader meaning to these activities. In
discussing prominent Irish building contractors in Philadelphia,
Dennis Clark has shown how they advanced their own businesses
but also contributed to their communities by constructing build-
ings that promoted group pride and solidarity—such as parish
churches, schools, and other institutions. The careers of men like
James McNichol moved back and forth between politics and business quite easily.[24]

The best (as well as the most entertaining) example of the
connection between ethnic politics and the entrepreneurial men-
tality, however, comes from that quintessential turn-of-the-cen-
tury Irish boss, George Washington Plunkitt. Although he would
have scorned any application of theory to his own behavior, it is
significant that Plunkitt described his upward mobility in politics
in strictly entrepreneurial terms:

> After goin' through the apprenticeship of the business while I
> was a boy by workin' around the district headquarters and
> hustlin' about the polls on election day, I set out when I cast my
> first vote to win fame and money in New York City politics. . . .
> Did I get up a book on municipal government and show it to the
> [ward] leader? I wasn't such a fool. What I did was to get some
> marketable goods before goin' to the leaders. What do I mean

by marketable goods? Let me tell you: I had a cousin, a young man who didn't take any particular interest in politics. I went to him and said: Tommy, I'm goin' to be a politician, and I want to get a followin'; Can I count on you?" He said: "Sure, George." That's how I started in business. I got a marketable commodity—one vote. Then I went to the district leader and told him I could command two votes on election day, Tommy's and my own. . . . That was beginnin' business in a small way, wasn't it?[25]

Plunkitt was content with limited mobility. He didn't want to be president, either of the United States or of a major corporation; he just wanted to be ward leader.

The corruption of bosses like Plunkitt was of a particular kind—intimately tied, for good or ill, to their local nexus of kin and community. Business and politics were intertwined, and both were connected to the task of providing tangible assistance to one's constituents. That is why, as Plunkitt explained, philanthropy was "mighty good politics."[26] And, in the end, mighty good business for himself, too.

Human nature being what it is, corruption comes in many varieties. A little vignette from the life of America's most successful entrepreneur of all—John D. Rockefeller—may offer a useful counterpoint to the building contractors and ward leaders who were quite willing to bend city councils and zoning laws for their personal benefit. In 1870, when Rockefeller formed an oil cartel called the South Improvement Company, he bluntly informed his competitors that those who did not join would be driven to the wall. One of these competitors was Rockefeller's own brother, Frank. John D. wrote him a letter, saying that "if you don't sell your property to us, it will be valueless." Frank refused to sell and, true to his word, his brother ruined him. Frank remained embittered for the rest of his life, even going so far as to move the bodies of his two children from the family burial plot, "lest they be forced to spend eternity with John D."[27]

The creation of the empire of mechanization known as modern industrial society required a single-minded devotion to economy and profit, a casting aside of all loyalties, even personal ones, that interfered with that goal.[28] There is a difference between this type of behavior and the community- and kin-centered motivations that, however attenuated, have traditionally been a part of ethnic enterprise in America, and no history or theory of entre-preneurialism that fails to recognize this fact can be completely valid.

## Notes

1. Ivan Light, *Ethnic Enterprise in America: Business and Welfare among Chinese, Japanese and Blacks* (Berkeley and Los Angeles, 1972). For a critique of this book's perspective on blacks, see William E. Perkins, "Symposium on *Ethnic Enterprise in America:* Review Essay II," *Journal of Ethnic Studies* 1 (Winter 1974): 73–82.

2. St. Clair Drake and Horace R. Cayton, *Black Metropolis: A Study of Negro Life in a Northern City* (New York, 1945), 430–69. The literature of black urban history is voluminous and burgeoning. Two other sources not cited by Light—both of which deal directly with the theoretical issues raised in his paper—are Sterling D. Spero and Abram L. Harris, *The Black Worker* (New York, 1931) and Abram L. Harris, *The Negro as Capitalist* (New York, 1936).

3. For example, Oscar Handlin, *Boston's Immigrants*, rev. ed. (Cambridge, Mass., 1959); Kathleen N. Conzen, *Immigrant Milwaukee, 1836–1860* (Cambridge, Mass., 1976); Theodore Hershberg, ed., *Philadelphia: Work, Space, Family, and Group Experience in the Nineteenth Century* (New York, 1981).

4. James Henretta, "The Study of Social Mobility: Ideological Assumptions and Conceptual Bias," *Labor History* 18 (1977): 165–78.

5. Conzen, 225.

6. Victor Greene, *The Slavic Community on Strike: Immigrant Labor in Pennsyl-vania Anthracite* (Notre Dame, Ind., 1968), 48–49; M. Mark Stolarik, *Growing Up on the South Side: Three Generations of Slovaks in Bethlehem, Pennsylvania, 1880–1976* (Lewisburg, Penn., 1985), 30–31.

7. Leonard Dinnerstein and David A. Reimers, *Ethnic Americans: A History of Immigration and Assimilation* (New York, 1975), 45–46.

8. Moses Rischin, *The Promised City: New York's Jews, 1870–1914* (New York, 1964), chap. 6; Caroline Golab, *Immigrant Destinations* (Philadelphia, 1977), 145–46 (deals with Polish immigrants); James Stuart Olson, *The Ethnic Dimension in American History* (New York, 1979), 215–16.

9. See Rischin, chaps. 7–12; Arthur A. Goren, *New York Jews and the Quest for Community: The Kehillah Experiment, 1908–1922* (New York, 1970). A good sum-mary of this trend can be found in Olson, 278–83. Deborah Dash Moore sees the second generation of Russian Jewish immigrants as contributing greatly to over-coming earlier cultural differences among New York Jews. Moore, *At Home in America: Second Generation New York Jews* (New York, 1981). Robert Tabak's forth-coming Temple University dissertation on Philadelphia's Jewish community be-tween World War I and World War II will explore this issue in some detail.

10. Olivier Zunz, *The Changing Face of Inequality: Urbanization, Industrial De-velopment, and Immigrants in Detroit, 1880–1920* (Chicago, 1982), 200.

11. The classic study describing these changes is C. Wright Mills, *White Collar* (New York, 1951). Alfred D. Chandler, Jr., *The Visible Hand* (Cambridge, Mass., 1977) describes the growth of managerialism in business in the late nineteenth and early twentieth century.

12. Zunz, 216–17.

13. Ibid., 357–58.

14. Ibid., 358–59.

15. Kenneth L. Kusmer, *A Ghetto Takes Shape: Black Cleveland, 1870–1930* (Urbana, Ill., 1976), chaps. 2 and 7, offers a comparison of trends in black and ethnic residential patterns.

16. On the decline of the older black elite, see W. E. B. Du Bois, *The Philadelphia Negro* (Philadelphia, 1899), 115–16, 119, and Allan H. Spear, *Black Chicago: The Making of a Negro Ghetto, 1890–1930* (Chicago, 1967), 111–12. On the shift from the old to the new elite, see Kusmer, 75–78, 191–95.

17. See Frank Furstenberg, Jr., et al., "The Origins of the Female-Headed Black Family: The Impact of the Urban Experience," in Hershberg, *Philadelphia*, 446–50.

18. Kusmer, 285–87.

19. Ibid., 194–95; Drake and Cayton, 465–66.

20. Mark Haller, "Organized Crime in Urban Society: Chicago in the Twentieth Century," *Journal of Social History* 5 (1971–72): 226–29; Jenna Weissman Joselit, *Our Gang: Jewish Crime and the New York Jewish Community, 1900–1940* (Bloomington, Ind., 1983), 138–39.

21. Haller, 211–16.

22. Arthur Paris, "Cruse and the Crisis in Black Culture: The Case of the Theater, 1900–1930," *Journal of Ethnic Studies* 5 (Spring 1979): 51–78. Benjamin McArthur, *Actors and American Culture, 1880–1920* (Philadelphia, 1984), helps place black theater in the context of a more general history of the acting profession in America.

23. U.S. *Fifteenth Census, 1930*, occupational statistics for cities; Joe William Trotter, Jr., *Black Milwaukee: The Making of an Industrial Proletariat, 1915–45* (Urbana, Ill.: 1985), 96–97.

24. Dennis Clark, "Ethnic Enterprise and Urban Development," *Ethnicity* 5 (1978): 108–18.

25. William Riordon, ed., *Plunkitt of Tammany Hall* (1904; reprint, New York, 1963), 9.

26. Ibid., 28.

27. Peter Collier and David Horowitz, *The Rockefellers: An American Dynasty* (New York, 1977 ed.), 23–24.

28. For the example of the steel industry, see David Brody, *Steelworkers in America: The Nonunion Era* (Cambridge, Mass., 1960), esp. chaps. 1 and 2. Robert Moses, longtime construction coordinator of New York City, provides an excellent example of an ethnic American who, in attempting to assimilate into the world of corporate, bureaucratic power, totally repudiated any affiliation with his own ethnic group. (He threatened to sue a Jewish encyclopedia whose editors wanted to include information about him in their publication.) In an interesting parallel to the Rockefeller vignette, Moses also broke off normal relations with his brother at a fairly early age, and after Moses became a powerful figure, he successfully prevented his brother, an engineer, from obtaining responsible professional positions in New York City firms. Moses' biographer found his subject's relationship with his family in general to be strange. "The Moses and Cohen (his mother's side of the family) clans were numerous; New York City was well stocked with his aunts, uncles, cousins, nieces and nephews. During his youth, it had been a rather close family. After he came to power, it was still a rather close family. But he wasn't a part of it. With the notable exception of the cousin involved in the matter of his mother's will, Wilfred Openhym, he generally saw them only on his own terms, in settings he controlled absolutely—at

ground breakings and ribbon cuttings at which he was both host and star. He rejected invitations to their homes. Gradually he cut off relations with most of them; almost invariably they ended in acrimony." Robert Caro, *The Power Broker: Robert Moses and the Fall of New York* (New York, 1974), 411, 600–601 (quote) and 576–601 passim. Of course, the type of empire created by Robert Moses was different from that built by Rockefeller. But the motivations and single-minded dedication were the same, and so were the results.

# 2

## *Ethnicity and Education*

### DAVID HOGAN

## I. Introduction

I have been invited to discuss the relationship between ethnicity and education under the general rubric of "Making It in America." "Making it," I suppose, is a colloquialism for what social scientists call status attainment: the relationships between family background, educational achievement, and occupational and income attainment. Traditionally, analyses of status attainment have involved two distinct but related responsibilities: (1) the measurement of precise empirical relationships between family background, educational achievement, and status attainments and (2) the specification of the causal processes or mechanisms that explain these empirical relationships.

What I wish to focus upon today is the latter question. In particular I wish to argue two propositions: (1) that although immigrant backgrounds influence educational achievement and status attainment, neither I.Q. differences, immigrant traditions, nor ethnic cultures can carry the major burden of explanation; and (2) that it is a mistake to look upon blacks, as is so often done in debates upon these issues, as simply another ethnic group and the last of the immigrants whose turn will come if only the government will stop interfering in labor market processes with affirmative action requirements and the like.

There can hardly be any question of significant educational and status attainment differences between blacks and descendants of European immigrants, although in recent years the situation has improved in a number of important respects. For example, in

Table 1

Percentage Distribution of Years of School Completed by Persons
25 Years of Age and Older by Race

|  | 1940 | | | 1970 | | |
|---|---|---|---|---|---|---|
|  | White | Nonwhite | Ratio Nonwhite to White | White | Nonwhite | Ratio Nonwhite to White |
| College |  |  |  |  |  |  |
| 4+ | 4.9 | 1.3 | .26 | 11.3 | 4.4 | .38 |
| 1–3 | 5.9 | 1.9 | .32 | 11.1 | 5.9 | .53 |
| High School |  |  |  |  |  |  |
| 4 | 15.3 | 4.5 | .29 | 32.2 | 21.2 | .65 |
| 1–3 | 15.8 | 8.7 | .55 | 16.6 | 21.8 | 1.49 |
| Elementary |  |  |  |  |  |  |
| 8 | 29.9 | 11.9 | .39 | 13.0 | 16.5 | 1.26 |
| 5–7 | 17.3 | 29.9 | 1.72 | 9.1 | 18.7 | 2.05 |
| 1–4 | 7.8 | 31.3 | 4.01 | 3.1 | 11.3 | 3.64 |
| None | 3.1 | 10.5 | 3.38 | 3.5 | 2.7 | 0.77 |
| Total | 100.0 | 100.0 |  | 100.0 | 100.0 |  |

*Source:* Ogbu, *Minority Education and Caste,* 173.

1940 only 1.3 percent of nonwhites twenty-five years and older in
the United States had completed four or more years of college,
while 4.9 percent of whites had done so; that is, the nonwhite
percentage was only 26 percent of the white percentage. By 1970,
4.4 percent of nonwhites had completed four or more years of
college, while 11.1 percent of whites had done so; that is, the
nonwhite percentage was 38 percent of the white percentage.
Thus, as table 1 indicates in greater detail, although the relative
position of nonwhites improved between 1940 and 1970, nonwhites still lagged considerably behind whites in 1970. We can
refine the analysis further by comparing the median number of
years of schooling completed by blacks with the median number
of years of schooling completed by descendants of the "old" (English, German, and Irish) and of the "new" (Italian, Polish, Russian) European immigrant groups. For adults between twenty-five
and thirty-four years of age in 1969, the median number of years
of schooling completed by blacks was 12.1, only marginally lower
than the levels achieved by members of most of the old and new
European groups (on average, around the 12.6 mark), but far

behind the median number of years of schooling completed by Russians (16.1), the great majority of whom were Jewish (table 2).[1]

The closing of the relative gap in educational achievement, however, is not reflected at all in income distributions. Unfortunately, I could not locate individual income statistics by ethnic group, but I did find income statistics for families by race. Eric Hanushek reports, for example, that between 1947 and 1974 the ratio of nonwhite incomes to white incomes increased from .51 to .62, a situation that left nonwhites, despite an 11-point gain between 1947 and 1974, almost 40 percentage points behind whites in income[2] (table 3). Thomas Sowell has estimated that as of 1969, the family income index of Jewish families was 172, compared with 62 for black families. At the same time, the family income index for the Japanese was 132, Poles 115, Italians 112, Germans 107, Anglo-Saxons 107, Irish 103, West Indians 94, Mexicans 76, and Puerto Ricans 63, and the only group to have a family index figure lower than blacks was American Indians, at 60.[3] In 1978, more recent figures show, the income of black families was still 41 percentage points behind the family income of whites. In black families with both husband and wife working the income gap was far lower, but the percentage of such black families declined very sharply between 1970 and 1978.[4]

Occupationally, blacks have fared relatively better than they have in income, but they are still highly overrepresented at the lower end of the occupational spectrum (tables 4 and 5). Com-

Table 2
Median School Years Completed, 1969

| Group | 25–34 | 38 and older |
|---|---|---|
| Old | | |
| English | 12.6 | 12.2 |
| German | 12.6 | 12.0 |
| Irish | 12.6 | 12.0 |
| New | | |
| Italian | 12.5 | 10.3 |
| Polish | 12.7 | 10.9 |
| Russian | 16+ | 12.4 |
| Black | 12.1 | 8.2 |

*Sources:* U. S. Bureau of the Census, 1971, table 13; U. S. Bureau of Labor Statistics, 1971, table 65.

Table 3
Median Income of Families by Race of Head, 1947 to 1974
*(Current Dollars)*

| Year | White | Negro and Other | Ratio Nonwhite to White |
|------|-------|-----------------|-------------------------|
| 1947 | $3,157 | $1,614 | .51 |
| 1948 | 3,310 | 1,768 | .53 |
| 1949 | 3,232 | 1,650 | .51 |
| 1950 | 3,445 | 1,869 | .54 |
| 1951 | 3,859 | 2,032 | .53 |
| 1952 | 4,114 | 2,338 | .57 |
| 1953 | 4,392 | 2,461 | .56 |
| 1954 | 4,339 | 2,410 | .56 |
| 1955 | 4,605 | 2,549 | .55 |
| 1956 | 4,993 | 2,628 | .53 |
| 1957 | 5,166 | 2,764 | .54 |
| 1958 | 5,300 | 2,711 | .51 |
| 1959 | 5,643 | 2,917 | .52 |
| 1960 | 5,835 | 3,233 | .55 |
| 1961 | 5,981 | 3,191 | .53 |
| 1962 | 6,237 | 3,330 | .53 |
| 1963 | 6,548 | 3,465 | .53 |
| 1964 | 6,858 | 3,839 | .56 |
| 1965 | 7,251 | 3,994 | .55 |
| 1966 | 7,792 | 4,674 | .60 |
| 1967 | 8,274 | 5,141 | .62 |
| 1968 | 8,937 | 5,590 | .63 |
| 1969 | 9,794 | 6,191 | .63 |
| 1970 | 10,236 | 6,516 | .64 |
| 1971 | 10,672 | 6,714 | .63 |
| 1972 | 11,549 | 7,106 | .62 |
| 1973 | 12,595 | 7,596 | .60 |
| 1974 | 13,356 | 8,265 | .62 |

*Source:* U. S. Bureau of the Census, "Money Income in 1974 of Families and Persons in the United States," *Current Population Reports,* Series P-60 (Government Printing Office, 1976).

pared with that of whites in general, the relative position of blacks improved between 1940 and 1970, but John Ogbu and others are surely right to claim that a job ceiling existed in both North and South separating black from white jobs. Nationwide, as of 1972, exactly 50 percent of blacks were employed as laborers, service workers, and factory operatives, whereas for the population as a whole the percentage was 38 percent, and for the German, Irish, and Italian ethnic groups, 36 percent.[5]

The theoretical task before us, then, is to explain both these differences in educational and status attainment and the changes in these differences over time. A comprehensive theory should be

Table 4

Nonwhite as a Percentage of All Employed Persons in the South, 1940, 1950, 1960, and 1970, and Index of Nonwhite Participation

| | Percentage nonwhite | | | | Index of nonwhite participation | | | |
|---|---|---|---|---|---|---|---|---|
| | 1940 | 1950 | 1960 | 1970 | 1940 | 1950 | 1960 | 1970 |
| Professional, technical, and kindred workers | 11.3 | 9.8 | 8.9 | 3.9 | 66.5 | 45.2 | 46.8 | 23.4 |
| Farmers and farm managers | 25.8 | 24.3 | 17.6 | 0.7 | 151.8 | 12.0 | 92.6 | 4.2 |
| Managers and administrators, except farm | 3.1 | 3.8 | 2.9 | 2.1 | 18.2 | 17.6 | 15.3 | 12.6 |
| Clerical, sales, and kindred workers | 2.4 | 3.8 | 4.1 | 7.6 | 14.1 | 17.5 | 21.6 | 45.5 |
| Craftsmen, foremen, and kindred workers | 8.0 | 7.8 | 8.0 | 4.5 | 47.1 | 35.9 | 42.1 | 27.0 |
| Job ceiling | | | | | | | | |
| Operative and kindred workers | 15.5 | 18.5 | 17.6 | 20.8 | 91.2 | 65.3 | 92.6 | 129.6 |
| Domestic service | 60.5 | 84.6 | 79.7 | 30.0 | 355.9 | 389.9 | 419.5 | 179.6 |
| Service, except domestic | — | 40.0 | 37.3 | 11.6 | — | 184.3 | 196.3 | 69.5 |
| Farm laborers and foremen | 47.2 | 41.3 | 46.0 | 2.9 | 277.7 | 190.3 | 246.8 | 17.4 |
| Laborers, except farm | 50.2 | 49.7 | 47.4 | 11.3 | 295.3 | 229.0 | 249.5 | 67.7 |
| Total, all persons employed | 17.0 | 21.7 | 19.0 | 16.7 | | | | |

Source: Ogbu, Minority Education and Caste, 150.

Table 5

Nonwhite as a Percentage of All Employed Persons in the North, 1940, 1950, 1960, and 1970, and Index of Nonwhite Participation

| | Percentage nonwhite | | | | Index of nonwhite participation | | | |
|---|---|---|---|---|---|---|---|---|
| | 1940 | 1950 | 1960 | 1970 | 1940 | 1950 | 1960 | 1970 |
| Professional, technical, and kindred workers | 1.4 | 1.6 | 2.3 | 3.9 | 41.2 | 35.6 | 41.1 | 59.1 |
| Farmers and farm managers | 0.3 | 0.3 | 0.2 | 0.7 | 8.8 | 6.7 | 3.6 | 10.6 |
| Managers and administrators, except farm | 0.9 | 1.2 | 1.3 | 2.1 | 26.5 | 26.7 | 23.2 | 31.8 |
| Clerical, sales, and kindred workers | 0.8 | 1.8 | 2.9 | 5.6 | 23.5 | 40.0 | 51.8 | 84.9 |
| Craftsmen, foremen, and kindred workers | 1.4 | 2.2 | 3.0 | 4.5 | 41.2 | 48.9 | 53.6 | 68.2 |
| Job ceiling | | | | | | | | |
| Operative and kindred workers | 2.8 | 5.7 | 7.1 | 9.4 | 82.4 | 126.7 | 126.8 | 142.4 |
| Domestic service | — | 33.9 | 29.3 | 30.0 | — | 753.3 | 523.2 | 454.6 |
| Service, except domestic | 15.3 | 11.6 | 12.0 | 11.6 | 460.0 | 257.8 | 214.3 | 175.8 |
| Farm laborers and foremen | 1.4 | 1.6 | 2.2 | 2.9 | 41.2 | 35.6 | 39.3 | 43.9 |
| Laborers, except farm | 8.6 | 12.9 | 13.2 | 11.3 | 252.9 | 264.4 | 235.7 | 171.2 |
| Total, all persons employed | 3.4 | 4.5 | 5.6 | 6.6 | | | | |

Source: Ogbu, Minority Education and Caste, 151.

able to explain differences in educational achievement in common causal terms,[6] and differences in I.Q. often lie at the heart of such theories. For a multitude of reasons discussed at length in the research literature, however, I.Q. differences do not seem to be anything like a sufficient explanation of individual, let alone group, differences in educational achievement, or status attainments, generally.[7] Well known are Arthur Jensen's claims that the mean I.Q. of blacks is about 15 points lower than that of whites on tests of abstract reasoning.[8] But the historical evidence that Thomas Sowell marshals against Jensen is compelling, although I rarely endorse any of Sowell's arguments. Essentially, Sowell finds that black-white differences in the level and pattern of intelligence-test scores described by Jensen are remarkably similar to native white-immigrant differences reported earlier in the century. Studies summarized by Sowell indicated the following average I.Q. scores in 1926: 83 for Greeks, 85 for Poles, 78 for the Spanish, and 84 for the Portuguese. Meanwhile, a study in Massachusetts showed that the percentage of black students with I.Q. scores higher than 120 exceeded that of the Portuguese, Italian, Polish, and French Canadian students, and other data indicated that Polish and Russian Jewish children frequently scored substantially lower on I.Q. texts than did children from other ethnic groups.

Early research also discovered patterns of immigrant performance on tests of abstract reasoning similar to those that Jensen reports for black students. Administration of I.Q. tests to Chinese-Americans, for example, showed that they did most poorly on tests of abstract reasoning ability, ranking them among the immigrant groups characterized by contemporary psychologists as unable to "master abstractions." Large black-white differences on tests of abstract reasoning are therefore in no way unique and do not require any special explanation.[9] The significance of these findings is summarized by Hurn:

> Taken together, this evidence allows us to conclude that there is no reason to invoke genetic difference hypothesis to explain the low performance of the black population on IQ tests. Such a genetic explanation was, of course, widely employed in the 1920s to account for the performance of immigrant groups who performed poorly on IQ tests. But as these groups assimilated into the mainstream culture, the difference between their test

scores and those of more advantaged groups diminished, and the early genetic explanations stressing the particular characteristics of their "racial" stock became both absurd and unnecessary. Since the pattern of black-white differences on IQ tests closely resembles observed differences between immigrant and majority groups earlier in this century, there is every reason to believe that such differences reflect not genetic inequalities between the black and white population but the persistence of caste-like social differences between races in contemporary society.[10]

If differences in innate intelligence are unlikely to explain group differences in educational achievements, what else can? There are several possibilities. Bowles and Gintis report, for example, that family background had a substantial impact on grades and years of educational achievement.[11] And there is a body of highly interesting ethnographic evidence that suggests that labeling procedures and teacher expectancies have a significant effect on grades and student aspirations, although not on standardized test scores.[12]

Yet another possibility, the "culturalist" explanation, attributes differences in educational achievement and status attainment to cultural, "values," cultural "deficits" or "deprivations," "cultures of poverty," and even, in a sinister echo of the rhetoric of social Darwinism, "cultural dispositions." Such views are common among academics and professional social pathologists. Thus, Milton Gordon describes the Jewish experience in America as "the greatest collective Horatio Alger story in American immigrant history" and ascribes their success to their cultural inheritance:

> . . . the Jews arrived in America with middle class values of thought, sobriety, ambition, desire for education, ability to postpone immediate gratification for the sake of long term goals, and aversion to violence already internalized. . . . It is these cultural values which account for the rapid rise of the Jewish group in occupational status and economic affluence.[13]

Gordon is far from a lonely voice crying in the wilderness. Nathan Glazer argues that upon arrival Jewish immigrants "were scarcely distinguishable from the huge mass of depressed immigrants, illiterate and impoverished" but that "they carried with them the values conducive to middle class success. . . ."[14] So does Marshall Sklare.[15]

Japanese immigrants are also described in similar terms. Indeed, for William Peterson, "even in a country whose patron saint is Horatio Alger's hero, there is no parallel to this success story," a fact that he attributes to the "civic virtues" of the Japanese— "education, diligence, honesty, competence. . . ." Thomas Sowell, as well, explains the success of Orientals in America in terms of what he calls their "human capital."[16]

The sorry state of black educational and status attainment, by contrast, is often held to be largely the result of deficiencies of black cultural values or traditions. Glazer, for instance, distinguishes between the immigrants' "slums of hope" and present-day black "slums of despair" characterized by severe social and cultural "pathologies" and "deficiencies" attributable, according to Glazer and Daniel P. Moynihan, to "weaknesses" of the black family that stem from the "legacy" of slavery and discrimination.[17]

Likewise, for John Hunt, one of the principal theoreticians of the War on Poverty, the explanation of middle-class success is to be found in the "rich" environment of the middle-class family and the "culturally deprived" environment of the poor. So too, in 1964 the Chicago Conference on Compensatory Education for Cultural Deprivation concluded that for culturally deprived pupils, "the roots of their problems can in large part be traced to their experiences in homes which do not transmit the cultural patterns necessary for the types of learning characteristic of the schools and the larger society."[18]

Obviously, efforts to explain group differences in status attainment are not mere academic squabbles but are innately political, for each in its own way underwrites or expresses a particular view about the nature of American social structure and history, the process of social mobility, and the appropriate direction of social policy. Liberal reformers link their arguments for busing and integration, affirmative action, compensatory education, and federal funding of educational facilities to claims about the pervasiveness of discrimination, inequalities of educational and social opportunity, and the cultural "deficits" or "deprivations" of the poor. Hereditarians, on the other hand, insist that any further social engineering is senseless because status is ultimately a function of I.Q., a genetic endowment. Above all, however, the Moynihan Report on the black family offers a classic illustration of the political consequence of a confusion between ethnicity and class.

By the early seventies, apostles of a "new pluralism" and neo-conservatives generally asserted that busing, affirmative action programs, and other measures to ensure integration or end discrimination violated democratic principles, constituted "reverse discrimination," trampled underfoot America's traditions of "social pluralism," and misconstrued the handicaps faced by blacks or Mexican-Americans.[19] For Thomas Sowell, the claim that blacks are the last of the immigrants and have suffered discrimination no worse than new European immigrant groups is a central component of his attack upon affirmative action programs and his belief that blacks would actually be better off without them: Since the Irish, Germans, Russian Jews, Poles, and Italians have prospered without government aids, then blacks can too. All that holds them back is affirmative action and the culture of dependency promoted by social-welfare programs.[20]

In the remainder of this paper I will argue that the culturalist explanations are fundamentally flawed and that blacks in America have historically constituted a pariah or caste group that has been subjected to special and qualitatively different forms of discrimination from those experienced by the New European immigrant groups, or, for that matter, Oriental immigrant groups. I by no means wish to deny that cultural factors influence educational achievement or status attainment. I do not believe, however, that they influence educational achievement in the manner suggested by culturalist explanations. Rather, educational achievement, whatever the racial or ethnic group, is a function of complex structural, historical, and cultural processes that can not be reduced to simple questions of individual ability, individual motivation, or "ethnic values." In the long run, differences in educational achievement appear more likely to have been a function of available education resources, opportunity structures, class background, race, and the shaping of educational "expectations" by the experiences in the labor market of the class and race to which the student belongs. I wish, in particular, to emphasize the significance of expectations or aspirations, since recent sociological and ethnographic research indicates that they provide an important clue, perhaps the key, to explaining group differences in educational achievement.

## II. Education and Status Achievement: Empirical Relationships

In this section I wish to develop three arguments: (1) that part of the explanation of black-white ethnic educational differences can be found in the systematic inequalities of opportunities; (2) that black-white ethnic educational differences have not been constant but have varied considerably over time; and (3) that the occupational and income returns of education for blacks historically have been consistently and significantly lower than for white ethnics. Then, in Part III, I shall propose a theoretical model that provides an account of how these structural patterns and relationships influence educational aspirations.

### 1. Black-White Educational Opportunities

A part of the explanation of differences in black-white ethnic educational achievement is to be found in the differences in educational opportunities available. New European immigrant groups largely settled in the urban North, but although a large number of blacks migrated to the North during World War I, until very recently the overwhelming majority of blacks grew up in the South. Because the South lagged behind the North in economic wealth, educational facilities in the South were inferior to those in the North, and within the South itself, expenditures for white education far exceeded expenditures for the education of blacks.[21] Moreover, prior to the civil rights era the situation for blacks in secondary and tertiary education was bleak.[22] In fact, most black colleges were little more than secondary schools.[23]

Measures of the gross differences between black and white schools—fewer school days per year, higher teacher-pupil ratios, less-well-educated teachers, fewer textbooks, lower expenditures, etc.—capture only part of the educational disability that blacks suffered under, both in the South and in the North. Most important, creation of this caste system of inferior and stigmatized education in the South reflected the widespread consensus that blacks did not deserve and should not get an equal education, for they were to be denied equal citizenship as well as access to all but the lowest service and laboring jobs in the economy. In the North such attitudes were less common, and the system of racial stratification in education less severe, but not so much as to represent a departure from the system of caste education. Not until the 1960s did efforts begin to break down the legal and informal mechanisms upholding the system of caste education in the South and the North.

## 2. Black-White Educational Achievement.

At the beginning of this paper I indicated something of the dimensions of black-white differences in educational achievement, comparing statistics for 1940 and 1970. Now that analysis needs to be extended to permit us to gain a longer-term perspective on changes in levels of educational achievement for second-generation members of immigrant groups and blacks.

Evidence simply does not bear out those who argue that the current gap between blacks and whites in educatonal achievement can be traced to the blacks' long historical indifference to education. During and immediately after Reconstruction the number of black children enrolled in southern public schools mushroomed.[24] In 1870, for example, more than 50 percent of black children in Arkansas were enrolled in school, compared with 63 percent of the whites, while in Mississippi 39 percent of black school-age children were enrolled in school, compared with 52 percent of white children.[25] W. E. B. DuBois quotes a report of the intense distress of blacks in Louisiana when, at the end of Reconstruction, the general tax for colored schools was suspended:

> Petitions began to pour in. I saw one from the planatation across the river, at least thirty feet in length, representing ten thousand Negroes. It was affecting to examine it, and note the names and marks (x) of such a long list of parents, ignorant themselves; promising that from beneath their present burdens and out of their extreme poverty, they would pay for it.[26]

In the North the evidence of a strong interest in education by blacks is equally remarkable. In an analysis of white ethnic and black school attendance in Philadelphia between 1850 and 1900, Michael Katz discovered that while the percentage of male children aged thirteen to sixteen from all white ethnic groups attending school declined between 1850 and 1900, the percentage of male black children jumped considerably. The effect of these changes was that by 1900 the percentage of enrolled black children (whether born in the North or in the South) aged thirteen or fourteen appreciably higher than the percentage of native-born children of native-born parents. In addition, the black percentage exceeded that of the native-born and foreign-born children of all the old and new European immigrants, with the exception of native-born children of Russian parents, but even here the difference was very small (table 6).[27] Also, Timothy Smith, finding extraordinarily high levels of school attendance among blacks in northern cities in 1910, concluded:

> The experience of urbanization brought out [among blacks] the values so long and so uncritically labeled "white Anglo-Saxon Protestant." No culture of poverty dominated the thinking of the early Negro migrants to Chicago, Philadelphia, Boston or Kansas city. The great mass of them wanted . . . the freedom and affluence of middle-class life. And they believed that the way to get them was to work hard, spend thriftily, build associations with other aspiring Negroes, and attend carefully to their children's education.[28]

All this evidence of remarkably high levels of black school attendance confounds those who argue that black educational failures today reflect and express a long history of "cultural" indifference to education. It also, of course, confounds those who, like Moynihan, blame black educational "failures" upon family disorganization, and that in turn on the "legacy of slavery." Not only is there no evidence of black indifference to education historically, but also there is no evidence that the black family was particularly disorganized either during slavery or during the early years of black migration to the North, as Herbert Gutman and others have demonstrated.[29] Moreover, there does not appear to be a close relationship between family structure or a mother's employment and either children's achievement scores or length of schooling. Stanley Lieberson found, for example, that "the evidence consistently indicates that a broken family is of little con-

Table 6
Percentage in School, by Sex, Age, and Nativity
1850–1900, Philadelphia

MALE

| AGE | | NWA/NWA | NWA/GER | NWA/IR | GER/GER | IR/IR | IT/IT | IT/NW | RS/RS | RS/NW | BLACK/NORTH | BLACK/SOUTH |
|---|---|---|---|---|---|---|---|---|---|---|---|---|
| 13–14 | 1850 | 0.63 | 0.59 | 0.47 | 0.44 | 0.31 | | | | | 0.37 | 0.32 |
| | 1860 | 0.65 | 0.56 | 0.57 | 0.35 | 0.49 | | | | | 0.68 | 0.43 |
| | 1870 | 0.58 | 0.52 | 0.56 | 0.30 | 0.37 | | | | | 0.57 | 0.68 |
| | 1880 | 0.61 | 0.44 | 0.57 | 0.14 | 0.58 | | | | | 0.62 | 0.57 |
| | 1900 | 0.54 | 0.45 | 0.42 | 0.00 | 0.50 | 0.31 | 0.44 | 0.49 | 0.72 | 0.69 | 0.56 |
| 15–16 | 1850 | 0.27 | 0.21 | 0.21 | 0.10 | 0.10 | | | | | 0.14 | 0.06 |
| | 1860 | 0.38 | 0.28 | 0.31 | 0.06 | 0.10 | | | | | 0.29 | 0.31 |
| | 1870 | 0.30 | 0.20 | 0.27 | 0.00 | 0.11 | | | | | 0.38 | 0.35 |
| | 1880 | 0.34 | 0.16 | 0.23 | 0.04 | 0.12 | | | | | 0.40 | 0.25 |
| | 1900 | 0.26 | 0.14 | 0.17 | 0.00 | 0.17 | 0.30 | 0.00 | 0.00 | 0.22 | 0.42 | 0.17 |

FEMALE

| Age | Year | NWA/NWA | NWA/GER | NWA/IR | GER/GER | IR/IR | IT/IT | IT/NW | RS/RS | RS/NW | BLACK/NORTH | BLACK/SOUTH |
|---|---|---|---|---|---|---|---|---|---|---|---|---|
| 13–14 | 1850 | 0.56 | 0.56 | 0.53 | 0.40 | 0.26 | | | | | 0.40 | 0.25 |
| | 1860 | 0.62 | 0.59 | 0.61 | 0.29 | 0.37 | | | | | 0.53 | 0.59 |
| | 1870 | 0.60 | 0.55 | 0.54 | 0.29 | 0.22 | | | | | 0.64 | 0.33 |
| | 1880 | 0.71 | 0.41 | 0.58 | 0.29 | 0.25 | | | | | 0.63 | 0.45 |
| | 1900 | 0.58 | 0.34 | 0.51 | 0.00 | NA | 0.189 | 0.54 | 0.35 | 0.42 | 0.50 | 0.50 |
| 15–16 | 1850 | 0.25 | 0.19 | 0.18 | 0.12 | 0.09 | | | | | 0.13 | 0.11 |
| | 1860 | 0.30 | 0.20 | 0.21 | 0.09 | 0.07 | | | | | 0.20 | 0.15 |
| | 1870 | 0.30 | 0.23 | 0.21 | 0.17 | 0.00 | | | | | 0.38 | 0.18 |
| | 1880 | 0.35 | 0.08 | 0.23 | 0.10 | 0.12 | | | | | 0.37 | 0.21 |
| | 1900 | 0.23 | 0.18 | 0.17 | 0.00 | 0.00 | 0.00 | 0.31 | 0.13 | 0.24 | 0.36 | 0.19 |

### Key

| | |
|---|---|
| NWA/NWA | Native-born of native white parents |
| NWA/GER | Native-born of German-born parents |
| NWA/IR | Native-born of Irish-born parents |
| GER/GER | German-born of German-born parents |
| IR/IR | Irish-born of Irish-born parents |
| IT/IT | Italian-born of Italian-born parents |
| IT/NW | Native-born of Italian-born parents |
| RS/RS | Russian-born of Russian-born parents |
| RS/NW | Native-born of Russian-born parents |
| BLACK/NORTH | Northern-born blacks |
| BLACK/SOUTH | Southern-born blacks |

*Source*: Michael Katz "School Attendance in Philadelphia, 1850–1900," NIE Project Working Papers no. 3, University of Pennsylvania, 1983.

sequence" for children's achievement scores, and that for length
of schooling, "family stability is a far less important determinant
of educational attainment among black children than their parent's education, and somewhat less important than the influences
of either parental occupation or the number of siblings. Indeed,
the combined effects of both family stability and parental occupation accounts for only two or three percent of educational attainment among black children after a variety of other factors are
taken into account."[30] Consequently, only a small part of the
black-new immigrant contrast in educational attainment can be
explained by differences in family structure or stability.[31]

The evidence, then, does *not* support culturalist arguments that
blacks have been indifferent or even hostile to educational
achievement, or that the differences between blacks and white
ethnic groups can be explained in terms of the legacy of slavery,
family structure, or female employment patterns. But this is not
all, for there is additional evidence that confounds the argument
that such differences were the product of initial indifference by
blacks to education. Lieberson has discovered that for those born
between 1885 and 1905 the gap between blacks and the new
European immigrants actually declined. For successive cohorts
born after 1905, however, despite the fact that the median
number of years of schooling of northern blacks continued to
increase, the gap between the blacks and the new European
groups began to widen, and widened spectacularly for those born
between 1925 and 1935 (e.g., for those between thirty-five and
twenty-five in 1960) (table 7).[32] This is an exceptionally intriguing
finding, for it both underlines the initial black commitment to
education described earlier and precisely locates the time—
roughly between 1920 and 1930—that blacks began to fall behind
second-generation immigrants.

### 3. Educational Achievement and Status Attainment

I have argued so far that black educational opportunities were
not only more limited than those available to white immigrants,
but inferior and segregated as well. I have also argued that despite
these obstacles blacks demonstrated an extraordinary interest in
education from the end of the Civil War on into the twentieth
century, so much so, in fact, that up to the 1920s they gradually

Table 7

Median Educational Attainment: Second-Generation Immigrants,
Northern-born Black, and Native Whites of Native Parents

| Cohort by Age in 1960 (and Year of Birth) | NORTHERN BLACKS | AUSTRIA | HUNGARY | ITALY | POLAND | USSR | NWNP |
|---|---|---|---|---|---|---|---|
| 25–34 (1925–1934) | 11.6 | 12.6 | 12.5 | 12.2 | 12.4 | 13.6 | 12.3 |
| 35–44 (1915–1925) | 11.2 | 12.2 | 12.0 | 11.4 | 11.5 | 12.7 | 12.1 |
| 45–54 (1905–1915) | 9.3 | 10.7 | 10.1 | 9.0 | 9.2 | 12.3 | 10.4 |
| 55–64 (1895–1905) | 8.4 | 8.8 | 8.9 | 8.4 | 8.3 | 10.4 | 8.8 |
| 65–74 (1885–1895) | 7.8 | 8.4 | 8.7 | 8.0 | 7.6 | 8.7 | 8.4 |
| 75+ | 6.8 | 8.2 | 8.7 | 7.4 | 6.9 | 8.2 | 8.2 |

*Source:* Lieberson, *A Piece of the Pie*, 163, 166.

closed in on new immigrants. But around 1920 or 1930, blacks, although they continued to stay at school for longer periods of time, began to fall further and further behind both the new and the old European immigrant groups. In fact, it was not until the 1950s that blacks once again began to close the gap. In this section I want to focus on what I believe to be central to the explanation of black educational failures since the 1920s—inequalities in access to occupational and income attainments for equivalent levels of schooling.

In comparing figures on educational achievement and occupational attainment throughout the twentieth century, it is apparent that black educational gains, both absolute and relative, did not result in commensurate gains in occupational status, at least until the 1950s. Even when blacks lessened the gap in educational achievement between themselves and whites, as the cohorts born before 1905 were able to do, nothing came of it.[33] In Boston in 1900, for example, more blacks than immigrants attended school among the ten-to-fourteen age cohort and fifteen-to-twenty age cohort. They were not able, however, to translate this into occupational gains: In 1910 there were two and a half times as many immigrants as blacks holding white-collar jobs, and four times as many in skilled posts. Twenty years later, the differentials were almost identical. Comparing blacks with the children of immigrants shows a similar picture. In 1900 blacks in Boston attended school in roughly the same proportion as second-generation immigrants (89 percent versus 92 percent for ten-to-fourteen-year-olds, and 20 percent versus 23 percent for fifteen-to-twenty-year-olds, respectively), but whereas two-thirds of second-generation immigrants entered skilled or white-collar jobs, fewer than one-fifth of the blacks did so.[34] Finally, Stephan Thernstrom found that although blacks in Boston made "impressive occupational gains" between 1950 and 1970, these gains were not associated with educational gains, since the educational gap between the races did not narrow over the 1940 to 1970 period. The implication of these findings for Thernstrom was clear:

. . . the main point suggested by the historical record is that education, that cherished American panacea for so many social problems, has been a tool of distinctively limited use for aspiring blacks. The economic status of Negroes in Boston from the late 19th century down to 1940 was much too low to be explained as the result of their educational deficiencies; the progress made by blacks in the three decades since then was not the result of the educational gains they made in those years.[35]

Two very comprehensive studies, one by Blau and Duncan, and the other by Christopher Jencks and his coworkers, provide an opportunity to examine the relationship between education, occupation, and income using national data. Generally, Blau and Duncan found that while family background did exert some independent effect on a son's education and occupational status, the son's own education was the strongest independent variable (table 8).[36] Nevertheless, the occupational status of nonwhites was lower

Table 8

Simple Correlations between Status Variables for Four Age Groups of Men with Nonfarm Background

| Age Group and Variable | | Variable | | |
| --- | --- | --- | --- | --- |
| | W | U | X | U |
| **25 to 34 (age 16 in 1943 to 1952)** | | | | |
| Y: 1962 occupational status | .584 | .657 | .366 | .350 |
| W: Status of first job | . . . | .574 | .380 | . . .[a] |
| U: Education | | . . . | .411 | .416 |
| X: Father's occupational status | — | | . . . | .488 |
| V: Father's education | | | | . . . |
| **35 to 44 (age 16 in 1933 to 1942)** | | | | |
| Y: 1962 occupational status | .492 | .637 | .400 | .336 |
| W: Status of first job | . . . | .532 | .377 | . . .[a] |
| U: Education | | . . . | .440 | .424 |
| X: Father's occupational status | | | . . . | .535 |
| **45 to 54 (age 16 in 1923 to 1932)** | | | | |
| Y: 1962 occupational status | .514 | .593 | .383 | .261 |
| W: Status of first job | . . . | .554 | .388 | . . .[a] |
| U: Education | | . . . | .428 | .373 |
| X: Father's occupational status | | | . . . | .481 |
| **55 to 64 (age 16 in 1913 to 1922)** | | | | |
| Y: 1962 occupational status | .513 | .576 | .340 | .311 |
| W: Status of first job | . . . | .557 | .384 | . . .[a] |
| U: Education | | . . . | .392 | .409 |
| X: Father's occupational status | | | . . . | .530 |

[a] Not computed because requisite tabulation was not available.

*Source:* Blau and Duncan, *The American Occupational Structure*, 178.

than that of whites at all educational levels and remained so even when Blau and Duncan controlled for social origins, education, and first occupation. Moreover, the gap between blacks and whites in incremental occupational gains increased with educational levels. That is, although education paid off for blacks compared with other blacks, the more education blacks received, the further their occupational status fell behind that of whites with compatible education. In effect, relatively speaking, highly educated blacks suffered greater occupational discrimination than less educated blacks. After Blau and Duncan distinguished between native-born whites of native parentage and second-generation immigrants, however, they concluded that "in sharp contrast to the inferior opportunities of Negroes, therefore, the occupational opportunities of white ethnic minorities, on the whole, differ little from those of whites of native parentage. . . ."[37]

The analysis conducted by Jencks, using data sets ranging from Blau and Duncan's 1962 data set to a 1970 national sample, uncovered results similar to those of Blau and Duncan in the main.[38] First, whites obtained higher status occupations than did blacks with the same level of education, and, second, the estimated effect of an extra year of elementary or secondary schooling on occupational status is significantly higher for whites than for nonwhites, although the gap has declined since the early 1960s. But contrary to what Blau and Duncan had reported, Jencks found that for college graduates the situation was quite different by the early 1970s; that is, college graduation had become more valuable to nonwhites than to whites. This does not mean, I hasten to add, that nonwhites with B.A.'s gain higher status occupations than whites, for they do not: Whites with B.A.'s still get better jobs than blacks with B.A.'s. What Jencks's finding means simply is that nonwhites without college degrees are now at even more of a relative disadvantage to whites than are nonwhites who finish college.[39]

As discouraging as the relationships between education and occupational status for blacks are, the relationship between education and income for black men is even worse. Whites have consistently earned more than blacks at every level of education, although the gap has declined over the course of the past twenty years. In 1959 black men aged twenty-five to thirty-four with a high school diploma earned 67 percent of what comparable whites earned; in 1969 the percentage had increased to 75 percent, but by 1979 it had dropped marginally to 74 percent. For black college graduates the gains have been far more substantial: from 59 percent in 1959, to 68 percent in 1969, to 84 percent in 1979. Attending college has raised black men's earnings more than it has raised white men's earnings, but black B.A.'s still earn considerably less than white B.A.'s.[40] In fact, in both 1959 and 1969 black men with four years of high school earned less than white men with only an elementary school education; blacks with four years of college earned less than whites with only four years of high school.[41] It has been argued that these differences reflect differences in ability or quality of education received, but as Jencks reports, even when researchers controlled for scores on standardized tests, black men at every educational level fared worse than whites.[42]

For black women, the situation is entirely different. Between 1955 and 1979 the income of regularly employed nonwhite women increased from a level that was 57 percent of the income of regularly employed white women to 95 percent. Black women today at all educational levels earn about as much as white women with the same amount of formal schooling. Indeed, black women with college degrees earned slightly more, in 1969, than white women with college degrees.[43]

What then are we to make of all this? Are we to look upon the discrminations faced by blacks as regrettable but not unusual for an immigrant group in urban America? Are we to trust to the cold logic of the market to eliminate discrimination because, economists inform us, discrimination is "economically inefficient" and because the alternatives, chiefly affirmative action, constitute "reverse discrimination" or racism? Our view of these matters depends a good deal upon the explanation we assume of the processes that bring about these outcomes, and it is to these, therefore, that we now turn.

The conventional wisdom is that over time education has surpassed family background as the major determinant of occupational and income attainment. Blau and Duncan, for examlple, attribute their findings to a triumph of "universalistic" principles of "achievement" over "ascription" for all groups except nonwhites, particularly blacks.[44]

Explanations of this apparent departure from the principles of

universalism vary. One approach is to argue that even with comparable years of schooling, either because of the inferior quality of
the education that blacks receive or because of innate intellectual
deficiencies, blacks in general lack the cognitive or intellectual
skills that employers value and reward. Yet there is an overwhelming body of historical and contemporary evidence that indicates
that such cognitive skills are, at best, a relatively unimportant
influence on occupation status. Even with school attainment held
constant, cognitive test scores are not good predictors of future
occupational success, and for many jobs in the economy, there is
only a weak relationship between cognitive skills and satisfactory
job performance.[45]

An alternative approach to the explanation of the relatively
poor occupational and income histories of blacks locates the
source of the problem not in black cognitive skills but in the
failure of American society to extend the principles of universalism to blacks. There can be little doubt—at least there is none in
my mind—that until the late 1950s or early 1960s the existence of
a job ceiling and "Negro jobs" directly mediated the relationship
between education and status achievement. Since the late 1950s,
with the acceleration of the civil rights campaigns, and later the
implementation of affirmative action programs (Title VII of the
1964 Civil Rights Act and Executive Orders 11246 and 11375), at
least most of the formal and many of the informal mechanisms of
caste segregation have been removed, or considerably weakened,
although pockets of resistance can still be found. Overall, however, Thomas Sowell again notwithstanding, the evidence suggests that affirmative action programs have improved minority
employment among federal contractors between 6 and 13 percent, and dramatically reduced the income gap between blacks
and whites.[46] But despite these advances, blacks still do not obtain
the same occupation status and income as whites with comparable
levels of education, and the efforts of the Reagan administration
to undermine affirmative actions programs—for example, by
eliminating travel funds for EEOC investigations of violation of
Title VII—will hardly close the gap.

A third possible explanation depends upon a distinction Lester
Thurow draws between two views of the labor market: "wage
competition" theory and "job competition" theory. According to
wage competition theory, labor markets exist to match labor de-

mand and supply. At any given time, the pattern of matching and mismatching gives off various signals: Businesses are "told" to raise wages or redesign jobs in skill-shortage sectors or to lower wages in skill-surplus sectors; individuals are "told" to acquire skills in high-wage sectors and are discouraged from seeking skills and jobs in sectors in which wages are low and skills are in surplus. Each skill market is "cleared," in the short run, by increases or reductions in wages, and by a combination of wage changes, skill changes, and production-technique changes over the long run. The result, according to the theory, is that each person in the labor market is paid at the level of his or her marginal productivity. This theory posits wage competition, then, as the driving force of the labor market. It assumes that people come into the labor market with a definite, preexisting set of skills (or lack of skills), and that they then compete against one another on the basis of wages. According to this theory, education is crucial because it creates the skills that people bring into the market.[47]

Not the least of the problems confronting wage competition theory is that much of the relevant evidence is not consistent with it. Rather, there is considerable evidence that American labor markets are characterized less by wage competition than by job competition. That is to say, instead of people looking for jobs, there are jobs looking for people—for "suitable" people. In a labor market based on job competition, the function of education is not to confer skills and therefore increased productivity and higher wages on the workers; it is to certify their "trainability" and to confer upon each of them a certain status by virtue of this certification. Jobs and higher incomes are then distributed on the basis of this certified status. To the extent that job competition, not wage competition, prevails in the American economy, we may have to alter our long-standing beliefs about both the economic benefits of education and the ability of education to increase social equality.

The job competition theory explains why neither a free-market approach, nor traditional liberal education and training policies, have had the impact on minority incomes that was expected. In labor markets based on job competition the incomes of individuals are determined not so much by their marginal contributions to productivity in a color-blind market but by the distribution of job opportunities. Wages are determined by the characteristics of the

job, not by competition between workers, and workers are dis-
trivuted across job opportunities on the basis of their position in
the labor queue. Position in the labor queue is, in turn, a function
of the *relative* level, type, and quality of education received, and of
the pervasiveness of discrimination practices in hiring policies.

The difference between absolute and relative advantages in the
level, type, and quality of education has been illustrated by Randall Collins. If, for example, one group, A, has a relative advantage of three years of schooling over another group, B, then so
long as group A is able to keep ahead of group B's earnest and
dogged efforts to close the gap, group A will continue to have
privileged access to the jobs, incomes, and whatever else higher
levels of educational achievement give access to.[48]

The second factor that influences position in the labor queue is
discrimination. There are, of course, many forms of discrimination apart from the everyday malicious kind. Sowell and Jencks,
for instance, have identified a form that they call "perceptual" or
"myopic," in which employers, on the bais of erroneous ethnic or
racial sterotypes, hire employees of one ethnic or racial group
rather than another. Similarly, Thurow has identified what he
calls "statistical" discrimination, in which employers hire or do
not hire on the basis of accurate rather than inaccurate ethnic
stereotypes. In this case, whether the employers are hostile to
blacks or not, they will not hire or promote blacks with educational
credentials and skills equivalent to those of whites because evidence shows that, in general, the education blacks receive is inferior to that received by whites.[49]

The political implications of all this are fairly obvious: Neither
the do-nothingism advocated by free-market ideologues nor conventional educational and training programs will significantly alter the position of blacks in the labor queue or the social position
of blacks generally. That is not to say that such training programs
are unnecessary: it is only to claim that they are insufficient. What
is also necessary and, I would argue, morally and constitutionally
required, are persistent efforts to improve the level and quality of
black education, to extend and improve job opportunities for
everyone but for blacks particularly, and to ensure equal pay, not
just for equal work, but for equal education. In time, such policies
would surely undermine the pervasiveness of both "myopic" and
"statistical" discrimination, help break the psychological nexus

between caste and black educational underachievement, and contribute to the equality of citizens that is a defining characteristic and moral imperative of liberal democracies.

## III. Explaining Educational Achievement

My basic thesis to this point has been that group-based "values" or "traditions" cannot assume primary responsibility for explaining differences in educational achievement and occupational attainment. Cultural factors are of critical importance, but not in the manner suggested by culturalist explanations—that is, they are not autonomous or independent causal processes. Rather, cultural factors, particularly in the form of educational aspirations, are significantly shaped by structural conditions. It is, therefore, in the interaction between structural conditions and cultural processes that the key to educational achievement is to be found.

Currently the most influential account of the significance of educational aspirations in educational achievement is the so-called "Wisconsin model" developed by Sewell, Hauser, and Featherman.[50] Nevertheless, this model fails to make a crucial distinction between aspirations and expectations.[51] In other words, the model fails to make a crucial distinction between "wanting" something and "expecting" something; everyone may initially *want* the same outcomes, but people at different levels of the stratification system learn to *expect* different outcomes. Pierre Bourdieu puts the matter thus: "Whether or not youths stay in school depends appreciably on their perceptions of the probability that people of their social class will succeed academically . . . there is a close correlation between *subjective hopes* and *objective chances,* the latter tending to effectively modify attitudes and behavior by working through the former! Children's educational and work ambitions and expectations are the structurally determined products of parental and peer group educational experience and cultural practice."[52]

I think by now it should be fairly plain what kind of explanation of educational achievement I have in mind, and a model of this kind has recently been proposed by an English ethnographer, Paul Willis. The thrust of Willis's argument is that, apart from questions of differences in individual ability, working-class children or children from minority backgrounds often do not so much fail to achieve but *achieve failure* through a variety of self-selection procedures. Willis proposes that school success or failure depends on whether students are willing to accept what he calls the "pedagogical exchange." The pedagogical exchange involves the exchange of good grades, promotion, credentials, and the promise of good jobs by the school for regular attendance, hard work, and proper behavior by the students. On the basis of their assessments of the desirability, possibility, and utility of good grades, promotion, and credentials, students work more or less hard, attend school more or less regularly, and behave more or less in an acceptable manner. Some students believe the exchange worthwhile; others do not. Those who do, succeed in school; those who do not, fail, or drop out as soon as possible.[53]

Two examples, one of black students in America provided by John Ogbu and the second an improvised account of Jewish educational success in America, illustrate the logic of Willis's model. For Ogbu, a Nigerian anthropologist teaching at Berkeley, the relative failure of blacks in American schools is an "adaptation" or "accommodation" to the caste restrictions and limitations imposed on black educational, occupational, and income opportunities. These caste barriers affect minority academic behavior in two kinds of ways:

> First, because caste minorities perceive their future chances for jobs and other benefits of education as limited, they are not so strongly motivated as the dominant group members to persevere in their school work. The perception of schooling as it relates to limited future opportunities may be largely unconscious for many caste minority group members, but it is an important factor in their relative lack of serious attitudes and efforts in school. Second, caste barriers generate or promote the development of different types of school- and work-related skills among caste minorities, as compared to the skills characteristic of the members of the dominant group. . . .[54]

Ogbu's major argument is that the high proportion of school failures among blacks is both a reaction and adaptation to their limited opportunities to benefit from education. In this sense black educational failure is not an individual problem but a historically evolved group solution to a group problem. In the face of discrimination parents and children adjust their educational aspirations to their caste status—they adopt expectations more in line with their caste status.

Ogbu's second point is more complicated, although the same feedback system is involved. His argument is that the cognitive, linguistic, motivational and other skills that dominant-group children take with them to school and that are reinforced there are "intimately" related to the kinds of skills required or promoted by the social and occupational roles they will play in adult life. But for caste minorities, the situation is both different and the same:

> It is *different* because their absorbed social and occupational roles require and promote different types of linguistic, cognitive, and motivational skills and behavior. However, the situation is the *same* in the sense that caste minority children naturally acquire the linguistic, cognitive, motivational, and various other skills or personal attributes adaptive to their adult roles. These skills may promote their failure in the dominant group's type of school success, but in that very way schooling improves their adaptability to the menial and occupational role they will play as adults.[55]

According to Ogbu, these attributes are "transmitted" to black children in the course of their socialization in the home, in the neighborhood, and in the school. The work of Willis Ray McDermott, Basil Bernstein, and William Labov also suggests that children from subordinate minority groups fail in school, or do less well than others, because such children refuse the identities, skills, and behavioral competencies necessary for success in the dominant society, and instead seek—or achieve—the identities, skills, and behavioral competencies that equip them for survival and self-esteem in the pariah or caste culture.[56] They simply refuse to interpret and behave toward the world in the manner expected and rewarded by teachers.

Unfortunately for historians, the kind of evidence that ethnographers can gather remains methodologically inaccessible. Historians are not able, therefore, to test Willis's model directly, but if we recall the data discussed earlier on the educational resources available to blacks, patterns of black educational achievement, and the severe caste restrictions upon black occupational and income attainments, then there is at least considerable empirical evidence consistent with a pedegogical exchange explanation. Given their occupational and income prospects, working hard at school and staying on at school hardly could have appeared particularly sensible to most black students. Moreover, black educational aspirations, as measured by levels of school achievement, began to decline in comparison with those of whites immediately following the institutionalization of the caste system—in the South, between 1890 and 1920, and in the North, during and after World War I. It was not until blacks entered manufacturing jobs in sizable numbers in the 1940s and embarked on the civil-rights campaigns of the 1950s and 1960s that blacks again began to close the gap with whites. Such historical associations might be accidental, but because we have good theoretical reasons to believe that the two developments are linked, the onus of disproof ought to be on the skeptics.

Let me now turn to my improvised account of Jewish educational achievement using the pedagogical exchange model. To begin, although Jews in America have been subjected to considerable discrimination, they have not been subjected to the kind of systematic discrimination meted out to blacks. They have not, and do not, constitute a caste or pariah minority, i.e., a minority whose position is one of institutionalized subordination and inequality in separate and specialized economic and political roles. Rather, Jews have constituted what athropologists call an "autonomous minority"—voluntary immigrants able to pursue, for the most part, whatever economic and political activities they choose. Second, Jews came to America with exceptionally strong backgrounds in the skilled trades and entrepreneurial activity and with established traditions of literacy.[57] Third, when they came to America, they were able to gain a foothold in the skilled trades and manufacturing in a rapidly expanding economy. Fourth, Jewish children, unlike black children, had access to the best public primary, secondary, and tertiary education that America could offer—although, it is important to note, Jewish school attendance and achievement was highly dependent upon class background.[58] Finally, Jewish graduates of high school and college, while often subject to discrimination, were not barred from the occupations of their choice, nor is there any evidence that Jews were paid less than other whites for equivalent levels of education.[59]

The educational successes of Jewish children cannot wholly, or even fundamentally, be explained as a consequence of Jewish cultural traditions of literacy and religious learning developed in Europe before immigration to America. Such traditions were important, but they could only significantly affect Jewish educational achievement in an environment in which the structural conditions sponsored expectations that academic success would result in occupational success. Without such conditions the Jewish commitment to literacy and scholastic application would have counted for very little. Educational achievement is not just an individual affair, or even an "ethnic affair," but a complex historical and cultural process in which the historical experience of groups, the character of available opportunity structures and educational resources, and the existence and extent of caste segregation all play a part.

## IV. Conclusion

In summary, then, what can we conclude about the relationship between ethnicity and educational achievement? Two points, I think, stand out. First, it makes little or no sense to look upon educational achievement as a matter of ethnic values, a matter of group differences in intelligence, or as a simple matter of individual ability and motivation. Rather, it makes much more sense to conceive of educational achievement as a complex cultural and historical process profoundly shaped by a variety of structural factors. Thus, while immigrant educational traditions and aspirations influenced initial levels of educational achievement, in the long run differences in educational achievement appear more likely to be a function of available educational resources, opportunity structures, class background, race, and the past historical experiences in the labor market of the class and race to which the student belongs.[60]

## Notes

1. Stanley Lieberson, *A Piece of the Pie: Blacks and White Immigrants since 1880* (Berkeley and Los Angeles, 1980), 128–32.
2. Eric Hanushek, "Ethnic Income Variations: Magnitudes and Explanations," in Thomas Sowell, ed., *Essays and Data on American Ethnic Groups* (New York, 1978), 141.

3. Thomas Sowell, *Ethnic America* (New York, 1981), 5; Christopher Jencks has criticized Sowell's figures on several grounds, but Jencks's own figures do not allow the kind of comparison I wish to make here. Christopher Jencks, "Discrimination and Thomas Sowell," *New York Review of Books*, 3 March 1983, 33–34.

4. Edwin Dorn, *Rules and Racial Equality* (New Haven, 1979), 30–36.

5. John Ogbu, *Minority Education and Caste* (New York, 1978), chap. 5.

6. For reviews of the research literature see Christopher Hurn, *The Limits and Possibilities of Schooling* (Boston, 1978), chaps. 4–6; Ogbu, *Minority Education*, chap. 2; Lieberson, chap. 1; Jerome Karable and A. H. Halsey, eds., *Power and Ideology in Education* (New York, 1980), Introduction; Christopher Jencks, et al., *Who Gets Ahead?* (New York, 1982); Ray McDermott, "Achieving School Failure: An Anthropological Approach to Illiteracy and Social Stratification," in Ralph Spindler, ed., *Education and Cultural Process* (New York, 1974), chap. 5; David Hogan, "Making It in America: Work, Education and Social Structure," in David Tyack and Harvey Kantor, eds., *Work, Youth and Schooling* (Stanford, 1982).

7. See, for example, Hurn, chap. 5; Jencks, et al., *Who Gets Ahead?* chap. 4; Sam Bowles and Herb Gintis, *Schooling in Capitalist America* (New York, 1976), chap. 4; W. H. Sewell et al., *Schooling and Achievement in American Society* (New York, 1976), chap. 1, 2; Phillip Green, *The Pursuit of Inequality* (New York, 1981).

8. Arthur Jensen, "How Much Can We Boost IQ and Scholastic Achievement," *Harvard Educational Review* 39 (1969), 1–123.

9. Thomas Sowell, "Race and IQ Reconsidered," in *American Ethnic Groups*, 203–39.

10. Hurn, 131.

11. Bowles and Gintis, chap. 4.

12. See, for example, McDermott, and Hurn, chap. 6.

13. Milton Gordon, *Assimilation in American Life* (New York, 1964), 185, 186–87.

14. Nathan Glazer, "Social Characteristics of American Jews, 1654–1954," *American Jewish Yearbook*, vol. 56 (1955), 15, 31, 32.

15. Marshall Sklare, *America's Jews* (New York, 1971), 59.

16. William Peterson, *Japanese Americans* (New York, 1971), 5, 113. See also his "Chinese and Japanese Americans," in Sowell, *American Ethnic Groups*, chap. 2; Sowell, *Ethnic America*, 282–83.

17. Nathan Glazer, "Slums and Ethnicity," in T. D. Sheppard, ed., *Social Welfare and Urban Problems* (New York, 1968), 84; Nathan Glazer and Daniel P. Moynihan, *Beyond the Melting Pot* (Cambridge, Mass., 1970), 49–50; Daniel P. Moynihan, "The Negro Family: The Case for National Action," in L. Rainwater and W. C. Yancey, *The Moynihan Report and the Politics of Controversy* (Cambridge, Mass., 1967), 51.

18. John Hunt, "The Psychological Basis for Using Pre-School Environment as an Antidote for Cultural Deprivation," *Merrill-Palmer Quarterly* 10 (1964): 236; Benjamin Bloom et al., *Compensatory Education for Cultural Deprivation* (New York, 1965), 4.

19. Irving Kristol, "Blacks are the Last Immigrant Group," in Daniel P. Moynihan, *On Understanding Poverty: Perspectives from the Social Sciences* (New York, 1969), and "The Negro Today Is Like the Immigrant of Yesterday," *New York Times Magazine*, 11 September 1976; Nathan Glazer, "Blacks and Ethnic Groups: The Difference, and the Political Difference It Makes," in Nathan Higgins et al., eds., *Key Issues in the Afro-American Experience* (New York, 1971), 193–211. See also Theodore Hershberg et al., "A Tale of Three Cities: Blacks, Immigrants, and Opportunity in Philadelphia, 1850–1880, 1930, 1970," in

Hershberg, ed., *Philadelphia: Work, Space, Family, and Group Experience in the Nineteenth Century* (New York, 1981), chap. 14.

20. Thomas Sowell, *Markets and Minorities* (New York, 1981), chap. 6.

21. Lieberson, 149, 142–43.

22. Ibid., 145, 148.

23. Ibid., 152–55. On the history of black education in America see Ogbu, *Minority Education*, chap. 4; Louis R. Harlan, *Separate and Unequal* (New York, 1969); Alan Bullock, *A History of Negro Education in the South* (New York, 1970); Judy Mohraz *The Separate Problem: Case Studies of Black Education in the North* (Westport, Conn., 1979).

24. W. E. B. Dubois, *The Negro Common School* (Atlanta, 1901), 43.

25. Lieberson, 139–40.

26. DuBois, 24, and Lieberson, 139

27. Michael Katz, "School Attendance in Philadelphia, 1850–1900," NIE Project Working Papers no. 3, University of Pennsylvania, 1983.

28. Timothy L. Smith, "Immigrant Social Aspirations and American Education, 1880–1930," *American Quarterly* 51 (Fall 1969): 523–43; and "Native Blacks and Foreign Whites: Varying Responses to Educational Opportunity in America, 1880–1950," *Perspectives in American History* 6: 309–35.

29. Stephen Steinberg, *The Ethnic Myth: Race, Ethnicity and Class in America* (Boston, 1981), 135–36.

30. Lieberson, 180–81.

31. Ibid., 186.

32. Ibid., 200–206.

33. Compare, for example, the figures reported in chaps. 6 and 7 with those in chaps. 10 and 11 of Lieberson.

34. Stephan Thernstrom, *The Other Bostonians* (Cambridge, Mass., 1973), 204.

35. Ibid.

36. Peter Blau and Otis Duncan, *The American Occupational Structure* (New York, 1967), chap. 5.

37. Ibid., 209–12, 233.

38. Jencks et al., *Who Gets Ahead?*, 213–14.

39. Ibid., 174.

40. Jencks, "Discrimination," 36; Jencks, et al., *Who Gets Ahead?*, 192–98; Hanushek, 144–62.

41. Ogbu, *Minority Education*, 174–75.

42. Jencks, "Discrimination," 36.

43. Ibid., 37.

44. Blau and Duncan, chaps. 29, 30.

45. Jencks, et al., *Who Gets Ahead?*, 225; Bowles and Gintis, chaps. 4, 5; Ivar Berg, *Education and Jobs* (Boston, 1971); Harry Braverman *Labor and Monopoly Capital* (New York, 1974).

46. Jencks, "Discrimination," 12–13.

47. Lester Thurow, "Education and Economic Equality," *The Public Interest*, 1972.

48. Randall Collins, "Functional and Conflict Theories of Educational Expansion," *American Sociological Review* 36 (1971): 1002–19.

49. Jencks, "Discrimination."

50. William H. Sewell and Robert M. Hauser, eds., *Schooling and Achievement in American Society* (New York, 1976), 20.

51. Alan Kerchkoff, "The Status Attainment Process: Socialization or Alloca-

tion," *Social Forces* 55 (1976): 361–81.

52. Pierre Bourdieu and Jean-Claude Passerman, *Reproduction in Education, Society and Culture* (Beverly Hills, 1977).

53. Paul Willis, *Learning to Labor* (London, 1977), pt. 1.

54. Ogbu, *Minority Education*, 41.

55. Ibid.

56. Willis; Ogbu, *Minority Education*, chap. 6; John Ogbu, *The Next Generation*, (New York, 1971), chaps. 4, 5; McDermott; Basil Bernstein, *Class, Codes, and Control* (London, 1973). William Labov, "The Logic of Nonstandard English," in Nikki Keddie, ed., *The Myth of Cultural Deprivation* (London, 1973).

57. Alice Kessler Harris and Virginia Yans McLaughlin, "European Immigrant Groups" in Sowell, *American Ethnic Groups,* chap. 4.

58. Steinberg, chap. 5, reviews some of the evidence. The Philadelphia History of Education Project has found similar results; see also Harris and McLaughlin.

59. Steinberg, chap. 5.

60. For a discussion of related issues, see my "Education and Class Formation: The Peculiarities of the Americans," in Michael Apple, ed., *Cultural and Economic Reproduction in Education* (London, 1982).

# "Ethnicity and Education": A Comment

## Mark Hutter

A growing body of sociological thought has begun to take issue with the long-held view that the best way to study ethnic groups and the assimilation process is to focus on cultural characteristics, i.e., the values and motivational systems, family and kinship groupings, voluntary associations, ethnic churches, ethnic neighborhoods, and their relative adaptiveness. Critics now observe that this emphasis on cultural primacy has tended to ignore social structural factors, such as the nature of the local, regional, or national economy, occupational opportunities, labor force characteristics, job locations, transportation facilities, and discriminational factors, in accounting for or explaining the "making it in America" of a given ethnic group. At the popular level, the results have been, for those groups that have made it, a self-congratulatory pat on the back, and for those groups that have not, only self-recrimination.

Even more acute for those groups that have not made it, however, have been the political implications of this framework's failure to deal adequately with social structural factors. All too frequently, simplistic models such as the infamous "culture of poverty" approach have linked the presence or absence of educational achievement and occupation status attainment to inherent cultural values and motivational schemata that virtually ignore broader social factors. The outcome has been aptly labeled a "blaming the victim" ideology.

David Hogan's paper systematically examines the inherent problems, biases, and flaws of the cultural explanations that have been applied to the educational achievement and status attainment differences of blacks and new European immigrant groups. Hogan also argues that the "last of the immigrants" thesis is open to serious question and that it would be more appropriate to view the historical condition of blacks in America as that of a pariah or caste group. Quite correctly, I believe, he maintains that blacks have been subjected to a form of discrimination qualitatively different from that experienced by white ethnic and Oriental immigrant groups.

Hogan's account of the educational and occupational experiences of blacks in twentieth-century America is strongly influenced by the work of Stanley Lieberson, Theodore Hershberg, Christopher Jencks, and others. These authors stress the social structural factors, or what Hershberg has called the "opportunity structure," meaning the availability of occupations and the spatial distribution of jobs, housing, and transportation that influence the opportunities open to blacks and other groups. Their research clearly demonstrates, as Hogan persuasively points out, that racism and discrimination played a powerful and instrumental role in denying blacks equal access.

Hogan's discussion itself incorporates education as a third significant structural condition, along with occupation and residence. Here again he clearly demonstrates that educational achievement and/or failure can best be seen in terms of complex cultural and structural processes and not simply in terms of individual ability, motivation, or "ethnic values." In this analysis, the three key factors accounting for educational achievement are (1) the level and nature of the educational facilities available to students; (2) the extent and nature of differentiating mechanisms within the school; and (3) the history of group adaptations or accommodations to available educational and occupational achievements.

Rightly discounting the argument of those who seek to explain the differences in educational achievement in terms of alleged differences in intellectual ability between blacks and whites, Hogan is particularly taken with a third approach that anthropologists, ethnographers, and, I must add, symbolic interactionists use to examine how symbolic, pedagogical, and political social processes within the school contribute to educational success and failure. He shows, for example, that ascriptive factors such as ethnicity, race, and socioeconomic status influence curriculum or track placement, and that placement, in turn, affects educational achievement.

Hogan discusses in even more detail Paul Willis's concept of the "pedagogical exchange"; that is, receiving the educational criteria for making it—good grades, promotions, credentials, and job prospects—in return for playing by the rules of the academic game—regular attendance, hard work, and proper behavior. This analytical model is illustrated by two cases. The first is John Ogbu's ethnographic work, which sees the educational failure of blacks as an accommodation to their limited future opportunities, the result of their developing different cognitive, linguistic, motivational, and other skills compatible with their future prospects in the caste society. Thus, Hogan suggests that the educational failure of students from subordinate minority groups is not merely the result of ascription or of cognitive mismatches with middle-class teachers but also a product of their failure to accept the "pedagogical exchange." They realize that the severe limitations of future opportunities make the trade-off unrealistic and even dangerous for them. In sum, the educational failures of children from caste or pariah minorities occur because such children "refuse the identities, skills, and behavioral competencies necessary for success in the dominant society, and instead seek—or achieve—the identities, skills, and behavioral competencies that equip them for survival and self-esteem in the pariah or caste culture."

The second and contrasting application of Willis's model involves the success of Jewish students in American schools during the early twentieth century. In that case, the Jewish tradition of literacy and scholastic application is combined with such positive structural conditions as openings in opportunity structures, responsible educational facilities, and prior parental records of economic success to foster the expectation that the pedagogical exchange would prove socially and economically worthwhile, as indeed it did.

Building on this historical analysis, which obviously challenges the "last of the immigrants" notion, Hogan then proceeds to look at more recent patterns of education and status attainment for blacks in the larger context of affirmative action policies, continued discriminatory patterns, and job competition theory. Essentially, the examination adds weight to his previous interpretation.

In reflecting on the points suggested by Hogan's paper, I agree that the predominant conceptual framework used in the study of

ethnicity and assimilation relies too heavily on the cultural characteristics of ethnic groups and is theoretically weak in the incorpo-
ration of social structure in the overall analysis. In contrast,
however, the approach rapidly emerging in the study of race and
assimilation, particularly in the case of blacks and Hispanics, relies
heavily on class theory. Undoubtedly the political and ideological
implications of the study and analysis of race and ethnicity patterns in the United States account for much of this new approach.
But in any event, there is a need to develop a more comprehensive theoretical model incorporating both social structure and
culture, and Hogan's analysis of ethnicity and education is a step
in this direction.

Nevertheless, I would like to see additional research and some
refinement of Hogan's theoretical model. Specifically, in the historical analysis of the relationship of blacks with the educational
and occupational institutions of this society, I would hope that
future research would examine intrablack differences. For example, we need to know how the voluntary institutions, churches,
family and kinship groupings, neighborhoods and communities
of different black social classes experienced and dealt with dif-
ferential opportunity structures. It would be most significant in
this regard to compare the differences in educational achievements and occupational and income attainments among the various black social classes. Furthermore, Hogan's data suggest the
importance of research on the differing experiences of black men
and women.

Future research should also be directed at interethnic variations. I fully appreciate that it was not Hogan's intention to examine these variations. But his perspective may lead some of us to
the wrong impression that all ethnics are alike and that their
historical assimilation process was structured by similar social arrangements and relationships, similar opportunity structures,
similar distributions of educational opportunities, and other aspects of the stratification systems. This, of course, was not the case.
For example, a comparison of the profoundly different experiences of Italian and Jewish children in American public schools
would document this, for different cultural and economic determinants played a decisive role in their respective educational
experiences during the first half of the twentieth century. As

Hogan has already looked at the Jewish student, I would like briefly to compare him/her with the Italian one.

Italian students were viewed by school personnel as more unruly and irresponsible than their Jewish counterparts when they both were newly arrived immigrants at the turn of the century. Truancy was not uncommon; many of the children were not in school because they were working. In fact, Italians had an appreciably higher number of their children in the work force than did any other ethnic group. Attendance in secondary school or college was rare. In general, Italian children were viewed as problems—difficult to discipline, slow to learn academic skills, and quick to flee the classroom for outside jobs.

The explanation that is frequently offered for this behavior pattern cites the significance attached to work by the students' parents and the disdain they showed for the value of education. Richard Gambino in *Blood of My Blood* states that for the *contadino*, the Italian peasant, education meant learning proper behavior toward one's elders and did not refer to formal schooling. According to Leonard Covello in his comprehensive study, *The Social Background of the Italo-American School Child*, there were many aspects of southern Italian culture and society that contributed to the Italian child's resistance to American education. In southern Italy and Sicily schooling had very little relationship to material success, and this view carried over to America. Indeed, as Stephen Steinberg observes, this attitude toward education also applied to conditions of Italian life in this country. A child's chances of reaching college were slim, and the likelihood of occupational and status achievement was not dependent upon school performance. Likewise, Covello describes the Italian-Americans' belief that education was a process of indoctrination into an alien culture that would destroy family unity, break down accepted social patterns, and jeopardize the role of parents as the prime socializing agents for future occupational involvement. Finally, most Italian immigrants lacked a concept of adolescence and simply believed that children from the age of twelve on had a responsibility to contribute to the economic needs of the household, the compulsory education laws notwithstanding.

Paradoxically, the negative reaction of American educators served to reinforce the totality of this belief system and the consequent behavior of the Italian student. In contrast to the Jewish student, who was usually placed in the higher-ranked academic curriculum track, the Italian student was tracked into either lower-ranked academic programs or nonacademic programs that included general, vocational, and commercial subjects. Thus, school officials had low expectations regarding the Italian student, and while they may not explicitly have prevented Italian students from achieving success in school, they did virtually nothing to encourage them. The result was a self-fulfilling prophecy that made it easier for Jewish children to succeed in school and made it more difficult for the Italians. Only after World War II, when the occupational structure and opportunities began to change, was there an appreciable change in the education achievement rate of Italian youngsters. In short, although more detailed comparative research is necessary, this illustration suggests that further study is likely to show the efficacy of David Hogan's comprehensive approach to ethnicity and education.

# "Ethnicity and Education": A Comment

## Henry N. Drewry

In my role as commentator I prefer to raise several questions with the hope that they can serve as a starting point for additional thoughts and other questions that can add to our understanding of the topic under consideration. Among the questions I would ask are the following: Is the subject of David Hogan's study worthy of his scholarly time and effort? Has he used the appropriate materials and obtained the most from them? Has his handling of the material contributed to our increased understanding of the relationship between ethnicity and education?

First, is the relationship between ethnicity and education a worthy subject for study? The answer to this is an emphatic yes. We have witnessed in the last few years a resurgence of ethnicity in which native-born Americans have increased the stress they place on their cultural relationships to their ancestral homelands—the countries of their parents', grandparents', or great-grandparents' birth. In addition, there is in the country at the present time a significant number of foreign-born for whom the cultural contacts with another country are a very recent part of their experience. In my state of New Jersey that number, according to the 1980 census, was 757,882 or 10.3 percent of the population. This percentage is down from the 23.5 percent of the New Jersey population that was foreign-born in 1920, and is about 2 points below the percentage of blacks in the New Jersey population in 1980. These demographic data, coupled with the historic position education has occupied (not to mention the extent to which it draws on the material resources of the nation), can leave no doubt as to the worthiness of this topic.

The first question, however, suggests two others that should be answered before proceeding. Is the relationship between ethnicity

and education an appropriate topic for the only paper presented
on the subject of education at a conference whose theme is "Making It in America"? And is the focus on black Americans an
appropriate one for addressing the broader question of the relationship between ethnicity and education? Here also the answer to
both is decidedly yes, even though Hogan makes no effort to
provide evidence of either, perhaps on the assumption that there
would be consensus on these points. I also suspect that he is on
sound ground on both matters. There are numerous other approaches that might have been taken to the topic "Making It in
America," but there long has been a widespread and, to some
degree realistic, perception of the United States as a land of
opportunity and of education as a vehicle for success. Moreover,
the measure of the mobility available in a society can only be
understood in terms of the opportunities available to, and the
limitations placed upon, that group or those groups who occupy
the most disadvantaged status position. At the same time, attempts to reconcile national ideals, on the one hand, and general
practices regarding blacks, on the other, have produced problems
of considerable significance, particularly in the area of education.
Examination of educational issues relating to black Americans
requires comparative information about nonblacks and, as developed in Hogan's paper, about the ethnic groups that make up
the white racial majority.

Second, has the author used the appropriate materials and
drawn the most out of them? On this my conclusion is somewhat
less enthusiastic. Hogan shows familiarity with sociological and
anthropological as well as historical sources. However, there is not
enough attention to the story of black education, especially to
material written by and about blacks before the 1960s. For instance, there is no indication that the works of E. Franklin Frazier,
Charles Johnson, Carter G. Woodson, and others were examined,
and the names of such scholars as Martin Carnoy and Ivan Illich
are likewise absent from the notes.

In addition, the study might have profited from attention to
black immigrants who came to the United Sttaes from other areas,
mainly the Caribbean. Making comparisons between the entire
black population of the United States (the vast majority of whom
are descendants of people who were slaves) and the small percentage of people who left one of the European countries to immi-

grate to America has certain obvious flaws. Yet this is not only what the supporters of the "last of the immigrants" thesis do; it is also what Hogan does, even though he clearly is at odds with those who see blacks as simply the most recent immigrants. One wonders whether it would be productive to compare black immigrants from the Caribbean with immigrants from Eastern Europe, and whether the results would add to our insight about race and ethnicity. Not much work has been done in this area, and while these oversights are important, they reflect only moderately on the fine quality of the sources used. For the most part, Hogan shows excellent familiarity with those materials published in the recent past that deal specifically with the issues of race, ethnicity, education, and status, and he has used these materials exceedingly well.

Has the handling of the material contributed significantly to our understanding of the relationship between ethnicity and education and the part played by these in "Making It in America"? Here again the answer is clearly positive, even though there are comments to be made on some of the paper's points and some of its approaches. Concerning education, Hogan puts forth two main propositions: (1) Although immigrant backgrounds influence educational achievement and status attainment, neither I.Q. differences, immigrant traditions, nor ethnic cultures can carry the major burden of explanation, and (2) it is a mistake to look upon blacks, as is so often done in debates upon these issues, as simply another ethnic group and the last of the immigrants whose turn will come if only the government will stop interfering in labor market processes with affirmative action requirements and the like.

The first point is soundly based on statistical data, but more attention might have been given to the historical factors at work. Clearly Hogan recognizes the existence of such factors, in particular the presence of "ascriptive processes" within the school. Nevertheless, the implications of this and other features of educational history may be more important to his overall argument than he realizes.

Hogan's second point challenges the conventional wisdom that blacks are simply the most recent immigrants and, if they possessed the abilities, would have moved into the American mainstream as have other immigrants. Although this notion has been an assumption (or an excuse used to justify inactivity) underlying federal government policy in recent years, it was expressed in earlier days by academics and politicians ranging in views from liberal to conservative. But its proponents never explained why the same group was passed over time and time again as one immigrant group after another "found its place in the sun." The theory could not account for that fact because it was itself flawed, as the information in Hogan's paper makes clear.

The most original part of the paper is Hogan's use of sources from the social sciences, as well as history, to show the nature of ethnicity and race in America, as well as the relationship of these to educational success status attainment. I question here only his use of the terms "caste" and "class." Neither seems to me to be quite the proper nomenclature for that form of social stratification that Hogan sees as the primary basis for the cultural formations in American society. Clearly class is not appropriate for blacks who have any combination or all of those social attributes that make for middle- or upper-class status, and the concept of caste usually includes both foundations within the political and cultural ideals of society for the setting apart of pariah and acceptance of their station by the outcaste. American ideals have been ambiguous on this issue, and one could argue that both political and cultural ideals for the country as a whole, at least during the last century, oppose the concept of caste. Historical evidence would also suggest that blacks as a group, like others who were discriminated against, never accepted that the way things were was the way they should be. Thus both terms seem inappropriate, and I would propose, instead, that use of "majority-minority groups status" would get us around several problems that are implicit in the use of the terms "caste" and "class." For all practical purposes, what we are talking about here is "race."

All too often, efforts to establish federal and state policies dealing with the issues related to racial minorities have suffered seriously from the improper identification of the problems and improper formulation of the questions to be considered. For example, the identification of weaknesses in the structure of the black family as a major problem to be addressed by government has tended to overlook evidence that family stability rests on the ability of men to provide support for families. Thus, government programs aimed at addressing family structure without taking into account job availability are certain to fail, and in the process are likely to lend support to those who claim that racial characteristics explain the problems of the family. In like manner, policies are bound to fail when based on the assumption that one or another ethnic or racial group is incapable of performing at a high level of competency or on the assumption that, if left alone, the market will take care of all matters as the "most recent immigrants" move inevitably into the mainstream of American life. Those of us fortunate enough to have read David Hogan's paper can only hope that it is read by others, including policymakers at every level of government.

# 3

## Ethnicity and the World of Work

### MILTON CANTOR

There is a whole range of relatively unexplored subjects sub-sumed under the rubric of "labor and ethnicity"—the manner in which newcomers of rural or peasant background adjusted to work in mine and mill; the effect of industrialization upon Old World cultural traditions; the influence of the Protestant work ethic and/or Americanization upon such traditions and upon the immigrant who entered the prefactory workplace; the impact on the newcomer of technological change, labor segmentation, and skill dilution; the development of the ethnic working-class com-munity or subcommunity and its institutions; the inter and intra-ethnic clash of cultures; the relation of immigrant culture to working-class awareness and solidarity; and the docility or mili-tance of the non-English-speaking work force largely unac-customed to unionization or confrontation with authority. To treat any one or more of these matters with the depth and density it deserves would burst the limits of what must be a brief presenta-tion, but I will touch on several of them in a speculative way.

Elsewhere I have noted the impact of industrialization on American society and, by implication, on those cultural values that the newcomer brought over in his/her baggage. It bears repeat-ing, however, that industrialization has redirected the whole course of human history and is perhaps its most fundamental process. Before the 1820s, when the transition from a prefactory to factory economy got under way in the textile industry, Amer-ica's economic landscape was dominated by rural culture and the rural community, with its relatively low rates of geographical and social mobility, its high degree of residential stability, and its relative equality—its "peer group society," as Herbert Gans called it.[1] Even the seaports and commercial entrepôts of the interior were "loosely connected islands."[2] And they, like the rural community, were comparatively free of immigrants and surely of non-English-speaking immigrants. Rather, they usually had a homogeneous occupational and/or ethnic character, face-to-face relations, and traditional social arrangements and institutions.

By the 1840s, the mills of Massachusetts had begun to attract English and Irish operators.[3] For example, Fall River was at first another small and sleepy town with a native-born work force drawn from surrounding farm areas, but the arrival of the Lancashire Irish helped transform it into a bustling factory city by 1850. Schuylkill County, Pennsylvania, was also typical, a region of cohesive little country towns mostly inhabited by the Pennsylvania "Dutch" until an invasion of Welsh and English miners, attracted to its anthracite fields, disrupted the region's ethnoreligious sameness.[4] After midcentury, the Poles and other East Europeans entered Pennsylvania's anthracite region, replicating the earlier process of ethnic displacement.[5] And their numbers were such that, as one Scranton observer noted, "there is scarcely to be found at Scranton a native of this country working under ground either as miner or laborer."[6] Luzerne and Lackawanna counties more than doubled in population between 1880 and 1900, and two-thirds of those working in the anthracite pits by 1900 were men from Southern or Eastern Europe.[7] The relatively homogeneous mine and mill towns of western Pennsylvania experienced more of the same.[8]

At the other end of the continent, at about the same time, there were comparable shifts in workplace and community ethnic composition. In post-Civil War California, for instance, skilled and highly regarded Cornishmen worked the diggings. They settled in muddy and dreary towns like Grass Valley, built neat cottages, practiced a devout Methodism, and won a reputation for initiative and independence.[9] Then came the Irish and the Chinese, replacing them in the pits and altering the community's economic and social structure.[10] Likewise, Yankee, Cornish, Irish, and, by 1900, Balkan waves settled in Butte, Montana.[11]

Little space can be devoted to the dynamic interplay of preindustrial immigrant values and those of the new industrial environment. But we must recognize that a dialectic did exist. At home the newcomers had experienced life as a continuous whole, a seamless combination of work and play, effort and pleasure. They had toiled on farms according to the weather, the length of daylight, and the amount of time it took to complete the chore, the season frequently dictating an accustomed rhythm of work. They alternated periods of intensive labor, such as harvest time, with periods of casual labor, when cold weather and shortened hours limited them to winter repairs. And even in town, the craftsman—as, say, in eighteenth-century England—knew an unpunctual life, filled with gossip and alehouse socializing one day and a dozen hours of work on the next, as he pleased.

Entering into American industrial society, the immigrants encountered the expectations and cultural attitudes of employers as well as native-born employees. For some, like English craftsmen, Puritanism had converted them "to new valuations of time; which taught children even in their infancy to improve each shining hour."[12] For others, America's employers or native-born fellow workers initiated them into socially acceptable attitudes toward work and management.[13] The impulse to work furiously for a time, owing to experiences of a peasant culture or deferential attitudes when an employer or foreman was present, was gradually eliminated.[14] In addition, American employers struggled to tighten up work routines, to dichotomize labor and play, and to frustrate habits that alternated periods of intensive work with boisterous play, tardiness, and scrupulous observance of "Saint Monday."[15]

Old World work patterns were not entirely lost, however.[16] Instead they were often buttressed by the development of an ethnic community that nourished and institutionalized traditional ritual and culture. Festivals and recreational activities celebrated homeland culture and shored up ethnic pride and cohesiveness, as did schools conducted in the group's native tongue, churches, fraternal orders and benefit societies, and the foreign-language press. For some immigrant groups, the attachment was short lived, but for others, self-conscious efforts succeeded in preserving a distinctive religion and value system.[17] Thus we may claim as normative for Worcester's Irish or for Detroit's Poles ethnic enclaves spawned by Yankee xenophobia but sustained over generations by networks of institutions.[18] And certainly we may assert that, in the early days of the factory system and at least for the first-generation American, Old World cultural ties were a power-ful, indeed the dominant, cohesive force.

In the rise of a new working-class community in the United States ethnicity was usually the major impulse that prompted residential clustering.[19] Lancashire cotton printers came to Lowell, Paisley thread spinners to Newark, German iron puddlers to Pittsburgh, Staffordshire potters to Trenton, Welsh quarrymen to Vermont villages, and Cornish tin miners to the lead mines near Galena, Illinois.[20] Moreover, they clustered in a particular locality or ward within a town or city, often on the same street.[21] They might, like the Italians of New York's "Little Italy" or the Jews of its East Sides, settle in groups according to the village or province from which they migrated.[22] Or they might use the entire town itself for a spatial anchor, as did the Finns who founded some of Minnesota's Mesabi range and Michigan's Gobegic range communities.[23] Understandably, then, in some communities, such as Boston's South End, only Irish brogue could be heard.[24] And where locality and job overlapped, as at Johnstown, Pennsylvania, and in Ohio's Mahoning Valley, only Welsh could be heard at miners' meetings.[25]

Whether immigrant workers entered into new communities or into wards already populated, they organized a complete cultural entity, comprising business, religious, and cultural forms.[26] They also established permanent residences, and many displayed a decided interest in home ownership, even at the expense of their children's education.[27] In so doing, they stabilized their ethnic blue-collar neighborhoods through several generations until other ethnic groups pushed their way in or structural change made the nearby factories redundant.[28] Some scholars have con-strued the preoccupation with home ownership as a sign of *embourgeoisement,* not a reflection of old-country culture, but the evidence is more ambiguous. The unskilled groups, such as the French Canadians at Amoskeag or Swedes in Worcester, were both most susceptible to radical political messages and least likely to buy a home and settle down. They were also most difficult to organize, however, since a minimum of residential continuity is needed for any sense of class solidarity.[29] In any event, whether homes were worker owned or rented from the mine or mill, employers encouraged the tendency toward residential segrega-tion.[30]

No description of the ethnic working-class community can be normative. In Lynn, Massachusetts, for instance, immigrants were assimilated with unusual speed into the larger community.[31] More often than not, though, the newcomers existed on the periphery of accepted institutions.[32] Thus, Johnstown, Pennsylvania's "hunkies," actually all Southern and Eastern Europeans and their offspring, were systematically and effectively excluded from participation in the city's public and cultural life—even from the better saloons and movie houses.[33] Newark's lodges, militia units, sports teams, and fire companies tended to recruit from only one class and one ethnic sector.[34] Nevertheless, a grudging pride in their own separate and informal structure of stores, banks, newspapers, and societies offered the excluded psychological comfort and emotional returns.[35] And the same pride, or ethnic identity, reinforced occupational identity.[36]

Such networks of separate institutions took in even the children who mixed "with everybody" and offered an important measure of continuity, a common bond, in the midst of growing change.[37] They might also, as among Slavic and Hungarian steelworkers in Pennsylvania, serve as a surrogate for unionization. Certainly they were less likely than unions to incur management's wrath, for they usually gave priority to ethnic rather than class interests.[38]

But we must be careful and most qualified here. Culture is seamlessly wedded to and interacts with the social structure. If we could interview an Irish Catholic laborer in Newark in 1880, and ask why his ten-year-old son had not attended school in the past year, he might tell us that New Jersey's public schools were insulting, that parochial schools were too costly, that the family needed the son's mill wages, that the boy did not need more education, and that the youngsters preferred factory to school anyway. The father would be baffled about which reason was most salient, or about whether he and his son were motivated more by "class" or by "ethnicity"—since all the factors reinforced the same behavior.[39] Working-class parents of other ethnic groups would offer similar responses. Moreover, workers might be distinguished from one another in still other ways—as craftsmen, as skilled laborers, as unskilled day laborers, or even as being of rural or urban background. Hence, even without factoring ethnicity into the equation, maddeningly complex differences can exist in working-class perception.[40] Ethnicity, however, cannot be ignored, for it too created important distinctions among workers.

The "old" immigrants, usually English-speaking or of German background, often formed one of the adversaries in nineteenth-century ethnic warfare. Frequently craftsmen belonged to an "organic community" of family and neighbors tied by reciprocal obligations of work and friendliness, and had entered occupations that utilized premigration skills. They either had brought with them, or had been absorbed into an artisanal culture that embraced ideas of cooperation, hard work, "manliness" and dignity, and the labor theory of value, as well as a residual heritage of Jeffersonian beliefs and, at times, the radical egalitarian and deistic ones of Thomas Paine.[41] Conversely, as representatives of that same artisanal culture, they opposed the menacing consequences of monopoly and manufacturing. In sum, the old immigrants enjoyed a pride in craft that enfolded a republican ideology.[42] But their view, rooted in a golden age of petty producers and commercial capitalism, confronted the profound social and economic transformation generated by mercantile and factory growth.[43] That industrial transformation was uneven, it must be cautioned, often slow paced and hardly sudden, for any productive process.[44] Generally, however, it was characterized by workers' losing control of the pace and conditions of work and then, in a process of circular causation, by artisan protest, replacement of the artisans with unskilled, often foreign-born, labor in increasingly mechanized factories, and finally by further protest.[45] Militance, often led by craftsmen, was an understandable development, as were a strident republicanism and ethnic tensions.[46]

That capitalism and its discontents existed is familiar; that ethnic-based strikes and violence should follow is no surprise. Immigrant working-class communities, we have suggested, *could* build cohesive class attitudes and resistance. They could confirm and strengthen a class-based movement—if the ethnic group was predominantly working-class; if, as in Lynn, it was integrated into the larger community; if it shared the same daily structures and work rhythms of other national groups; and if it had residential stability, which, as Marx understood, was a prerequisite for the building of class awareness.[47]

Collective awareness, therefore, at times transcended ethnic group boundaries and led workers from diverse ethnic backgrounds to interact—as did German shoemakers, Catholic weavers, and Presbyterian ship carpenters, who joined Irish textile hands in Philadelphia in the 1830s and demonstrated substantial labor solidarity until the 1837 panic destroyed their union.[48] A similar awareness characterized Chicago's stockyard workers around 1900,[49] Homestead's strike leaders,[50] Pennsylvania's ironworker unions,[51] and, for a while at least, the multi-ethnic mill operatives of Lawrence, Massachusetts.[52]

Certain ethnic groups even brought with them as part of their heritage traditions of class resistance. Witness, for instance, the Jewish needle trade operatives who came out of Lithuanian or Byelorussian tailoring centers, where they belonged to working-class organizations like the Bund and possessed a fighting elan that served them well in urban sweatshops, or the post–Civil War Germans who had been fed on the rebellious passions of 1848 and who adapted anarchist enthusiasms to the eight-hour-day campaign in Chicago in the 1880s.[53] Most Italian arrivals, to be sure, repeated the usual pattern of first-generation immigrant submissiveness to factory discipline and authority, but like the Irish and the Slavs, they could erupt in sudden outbursts of rebelliousness—analogous to Whiteboy violence in County Cork or the *fascio* in Sicily. Moreover, some of the most active union leaders in the Amalgamated Clothing Workers of America were southern Italians.[54]

Nevertheless, while many instances of cross-ethnic labor solidarity may be considered, immigrant rivalry over jobs, threat of skill dilution, and occupational displacement manifested in the division of labor led to socioeconomic dislocation and class fragmentation. Thus, ethnic clashes usually coexisted with labor conflict.[55]

Among the earliest of the immigrant groups, the Irish brought with them a Gaelic culture, Fenian nationalism, rural folkways and, after 1845, an almost exclusively Catholic faith. Here they undertook the most arduous work. They constructed Pennsylvania's canals and railways, as well as its iron foundries and textile mills, which they then entered. They also built Worcester's and Chicopee's canals in the 1820s, and the Lynn and Lowell textile mills, into which they were also recruited, composing a third of the workers in those mills by the mid 1840s. They flooded Massachusetts factory towns into the 1870s; swelled New York City's dock labor force and, invoking a weapon of their rural past, boycotted antilabor employers; joined the German influx into Buffalo and other cities in the 1860s; and, as in Jersey City, Lawrence, Detroit, and Cohoes, New York, filled the bottom ranks of American labor.[56]

Skilled workers, with a record of class militancy shaped by prior experience in English factories, Irish immigrants in Fall River, Massachusetts, helped to organize trade unions.[57] More typical, though, were those of the Newburyport and Lowell mills, who accepted low wages, menial labor, segregated housing, and factory work, and were even excluded from subsidized company housing. In short, the Irish usually occupied a dual track factory labor market.[58] They also catalyzed the anxieties of both craftsmen and nativists, who were at times one and the same.[59] So, almost everywhere the immigrants went, the menacing trinity of urban poverty, unskilled labor, and Irish Catholicism produced endemic violence—an epidemic of labor turbulence, political factionalism, and race and religious riots—from the late 1820s through the 1850s.[60] In some cities, riots even became integral to the activities of ethnic communities and street gangs, the latter being united by ethnic or neighborhood ties. Midcentury New York and Philadelphia, for instance, were racked by gang violence, much of it ethnoreligious in origin.[61]

The Irish, moreover, appeared to be hopelessly quarrelsome, as well as socially derelict. Refugees from famine conditions—usually landless laborers or peasant cottagers—they carried cultural traditions very different from those of their predecessors—often seasonal migrants out of English textile towns or prosperous farmers from the eastern counties.[62] Indeed, because Irish Protestant artisans were among those who felt threatened by the seamless web of factory production, technological change, job displacement, and Catholic invasion, intra-Irish conflict developed from the outset.[63]

Inter- and intraethnic labor tensions existed virtually everywhere, spilling over from the workplace into the larger community and even onto the national scene. The bloody battles of the early 1900s, when the Irish of Chicago's Near North Side sought to eliminate an Italian beachhead, were typical of an apparently endless number of such community conflicts—in this case between workers of the same religious faith and occupational stratum.[64] At times riots were fueled by other nonworkplace issues, such as the use of the King James Bible in public schools, tax monies for parochial schools, or the liquor traffic, and these clashes were frequently channeled into political alliances, further heightening social tensions.[65]

When national feuds broke out, as they did as soon as British and Irish miners appeared in Pennsylvania's anthracite fields, they were exacerbated by ethnic clustering, which there and elsewhere was reinforced by the skill and job/status hierarchy. At Carbondale, and throughout eastern Pennsylvania just a few years later, Irish (and German) resentment toward the Welsh and Scots who worked the best veins kept the ethnic groups involved at near-riot readiness.[66] Scranton's Irish coal miners and mine laborers received a third less in wages than did their Protestant enemies, the English and Welsh foremen. Reflecting the continual process of ethnic displacement at the bottom layers of the labor force, thirty years later the Irish were the skilled colliers and the newly arrived Slavic helpers were now the exploited.[67] Comparable developments occurred in virtually all industrial sectors, most notably in steel. At Homestead, for example, bitterness and anxiety characterized the process, and splintered labor's ranks, the skilled fearing the semiskilled, the semiskilled fearing the unskilled, and native-born fearing "foreigners" who were pushing into skilled ranks. Management played on such anxieties and ensured that each man jealously guarded "his work in the U.S. Steel estate."[68]

The process of ethnic displacement, almost always beginning at the bottom occupational rungs, was hardly limited to the mining and steel industries. For example, the English, Irish, and French Canadians, successively, were driven out of menial positions in the Fall River textile mills and often out of the mills altogether. Commonly they then joined their immediate predecessors and former antagonists in mutual hostility to the new menial work force.[69]

The parochial self-interest of many nineteenth-century unions—and not simply craft organizations such as the AFL or the Amalgamated Association of Iron and Steel Workers—is apparent in their refusal to recruit unskilled Eastern and Southern European immigrants.[70] As a result, the intensity of ethnic antagonism that divided and disorganized the labor movement in New York City, Philadelphia, Massachusetts factory towns, and the Upper

Michigan and California mining regions was a debilitating fact of working-class life.[71] Shifts in the ethnic composition of the working-class over generations, accompanied by modernization and industrial restructuring, simply intensified such reactions as, in many instances, did use of an ethnic strike-breaking force.[72]

Finally, because ethnic group interests were usually coterminous with family loyalties and family members often helped each other at the expense of other workers, in yet another and oblique way ethnicity "obstructed working-class solidarity."[73] The former peasants who worked in the Monongahela Valley steel mills displayed less interest in labor solidarity than in sacrificing all for the family, and Gaelic newcomers in the later nineteenth century were partly insulated from a strenuous individualism as well as class awareness by a strong sense of family.[74] None of this was entirely by chance. When companies hired, they often established ethnic and familial networks. Thus the Johnstown, Pennsylvania, steel mills resorted to "family hiring," and the Amoskeag cotton mill in New Hampshire utilized the workers' own informal ties by encouraging those already hired to recruit their French Canadian kin.[75] In turn, the work process itself contributed to ethnic and familial bonding. Much as the newcomer refused to join, or was denied entry into, unions or Protestant fraternal societies and founded his own, so he drew his own kind into ethnic-specific work situations. Family and kinship ties, then, functioned as hiring halls; and they also provided the focal point of personal life, as well as the basis for benefit society, political club, fraternal lodge, and parish church activities.[76]

In summary, we may conclude, ethnicity was the primary organizing principle in the immigrant and immigrant group experience. But whether it produced a society so highly fragmented that it was *never* able to unite around common goals and grievances is most doubtful. For whether ethnicity was the crucial deterrent to class awareness depended upon a multiplicity of factors, no less than variables in time and space, the historic specificity of groups and places.

## Notes

1. Herbert Gans, *Urban Villagers* (New York, 1962), 36.
2. Robert H. Wiebe, *The Search for Order* (New York, 1967), 4, 44.
3. Christopher Clark, "Household, Market and Capital: The Process of

Economic Change in the Connecticut Valley of Massachusetts, 1800–1860" (Ph.D. diss., Harvard University, 1982).

4. William Gudalunas, "Before the Molly Maguires: The Emergence of the Ethno-Religious Factor in the Politics of the Lower Anthracite Region" (Ph.D. diss., Lehigh University, 1973), 29–33. The best concise treatment of the social structure of the Pennsylvania anthracite region is Rowland Berthoff, "The Social Order of the Anthracite Region, 1825–1902," *Pennsylvania Magazine of History and Biography* 89 (July 1965): 261–91. On Welsh and English immigrants, see Wilbur Shepperson, *British Emigration to North America* (Minneapolis, 1957); Charlotte Erickson, *Invisible Immigrants: The Adaptation of English and Scottish Immigrants in Nineteenth Century America* (Coral Gables, Fla., 1972); and Rowland Berthoff, *British Immigrants in Industrial America* (New York, 1953).

5. Caroline Golab, *Immigrant Destinations* (Philadelphia, 1977), 36.

6. Samuel Walker, Jr., "Paternalism, Class Consciousness, and Ethnicity: Conflicting Influences on the Workingmen of Scranton, Pa., 1850–1885" (unpublished Ms).

7. Michael Barendse, *Social Expectations and Perceptions: Case of Slavic Anthracite Workers* (University Park, Penn., 1981), 3, 17, 20–21.

8. Carl I. Meyerhuber Jr., "The Alle-Kiski Coal Wars, 1913–1919," *Western Pennsylvania Historical Magazine* 63 (July 1980): 197–213.

9. Shirley Ewart, "Cornish Miners in Grass Valley," *Pacific Historian* 25 (Winter 1981): 39, 41–42.

10. Ralph Mann, *After the Gold Rush: Society in Grass Valley and Nevada City, California, 1848–1870* (Stanford, 1982).

11. Mark Wyman, *Hard-Rock Epic: Western Miners and the Industrial Revolution, 1850–1910* (Berkeley and Los Angeles, 1979).

12. Edward P. Thompson, "Time, Work-Discipline and Industrial Capitalism," *Past and Present* 38 (1967): 56–97. There is a substantial literature on the seasonal rhythms of rural life and labor and the rituals and recreation that filled the moments of leisure. See, for example, James Henretta, *The Evolution of American Society* (Lexington, Mass., 1973), 198; Hugh Cunningham, *Leisure in the Industrial Revolution* (London, 1980), 62, 63; and Michael Marrus, *The Emergence of Leisure* (New York, 1974), 75.

13. David Montgomery, *Worker Control in America* (New York, 1979), 43.

14. William I. Thomas and Florian Znaniecki, *The Polish Peasant in Europe and America* (Boston, 1918–1920), 1:199. On the English rural laborer, see Patrick Joyce, *Work, Society, and Politics* (Brighton, Sussex, England, 1980), 91, 94, 124.

15. William Sisson, "From Farm to Factory," in *Essays in Textile History, Working Papers from the Regional Economic History Center* 4, no. 4 (1981).

16. Montgomery, *Worker Control,* 40–43.

17. Clyde Griffen and Sally Griffen, *Natives and Newcomers: The Ordering of Opportunity in Mid-Nineteenth-Century Poughkeepsie* (Cambridge, Mass., 1978), 44.

18. Olivier Zunz, *The Changing Face of Inequality: Urbanization, Industrial Development, and Immigrants in Detroit, 1880–1920* (Chicago, 1982), Timothy J. Meagher, "The Lord Is Not Dead: Cultural and Social Change among the Irish in Worcester, Massachusetts" (Ph.D. diss., Brown University, 1982).

19. Zunz, 178, 180.

20. Rowland Berthoff, *An Unsettled People* (New York, 1971), 165–66.

21. Jeremy Brecher, et al., *Brass Valley: The Story of Working People's Lives and Struggles in an American Industrial Region* (Philadelphia, 1982), 7, 8; James P. Hanlan, *The Working Population of Manchester, New Hampshire, 1840–1886* (Ann Arbor, 1981), 183; Meagher, 402; Ewa K. Hauser, "Ethnicity and Class Con-

sciousness in a Polish-American Community" (Ph.D. diss., The Johns Hopkins University, 1981), 118.

22. Selma C. Berrol, *Immigrants at School: New York City, 1898–1914* (New York, 1978), 48.

23. Peter Kivisto, *Immigrant Socialists in the United States: The Case of Finns and the Left* (Rutherford, N.J., 1984).

24. David Doyle, "Unestablished Irishmen: New Immigrants and Industrial America, 1870–1910," in Dirk Hoerder, ed., *American Labor and Immigration History, 1877–1920* (Urbana, Ill., 1983), 216.

25. Linda Schneider, "The Citizen Striker: Working Class Radicalism in Industrial Conflict, 1870–1920: Three Case Studies" (unpublished MS).

26. Zunz, 193–94.

27. Ibid., 153.

28. Meagher, 425, 428.

29. Sune Akerman and Hans Norman, "Political Mobilization of the Workers: The Case of the Worcester Swedes," in Hoerder, *American Labor*, 250.

30. Kivisto, *Immigrant Socialists*, 86.

31. On the socializing of Lynn's workers in ethnic clubs and societies, see Bessie Van Vorst and Marie Van Vorst, *The Woman Who Toils* (New York, 1903). Networks of associations as surrogates for trade unions are explored in H. A. Turner, *Trade Union Growth, Structure, and Policy* (Toronto, 1962), 85.

32. Richard, Judd, "Socialist Cities: Explorations into the Grass Roots of American Socialism" (Ph.D. diss., University of California, Irvine, 1979), 37 and passim.

33. Ewa Morawska, "The Internal Status Hierarchy in the East European Communities in Johnstown, Pa., 1890–1930s," *Journal of Social History* 16 (Fall 1982): 79; Ewa Morawska, *For Bread and Butter: The Life-Worlds of the East Central Europeans in Johnstown, Pennsylvania, 1890–1940* (Cambridge and New York, 1985), 103.

34. Susan E. Hirsch, *Roots of the American Working Class* (Philadelphia, 1978), 100–101. In Newark, as elsewhere, societies like the Newark Hibernian Society and the Mutual Benefit Society of Mechanics, among others, included employees as well as employers: "all those of the same nationality." Ibid., 87.

35. There is a substantial literature affirming as much. For one example and quite representative, see Zunz.

36. Marcus Lee Hansen and J. B. Brebner, *The Mingling of the Canadian and American People* (New York, 1970), 18, 120–25, 160–69. See also State of Massachusetts, *Report of the Bureau of Statistics of Labor* 11 (Boston, 1880), 59 and passim; and ibid. 13 (Boston, 1882), 64, on the French Canadian practice of taking the place of striking English and Irish textile operatives. On Holyoke's French Canadians, see Kenneth Underwood, *Protestant and Catholic Century* (Boston, 1957), 211; Virginia B. Cunz, *The French in America* (Minneapolis, 1960), 81; Constance McLaughlin Green, *Holyoke, Massachusetts* (New Haven, 1968), 202, 369–70; U.S. Senate, *Labor and Capital* 1 (1885), 66–67. See also *John Swinton's Paper* (New York), 6 January 1884. Newburyport's Irish Catholics, a fourth of the city's population in 1880, had their own churches, parochial school system and social institutions; and this was a paradigmatic practice. Stephan Thernstrom, "Labor and Community in 1880," in Peter Stearns and Daniel Walkowitz, eds, *Workers in the Industrial Society* (New Brunswick, N.J., 1974), 185; Walker, 93; Kivisto, 120; Richard Parmet, *Labor and Immigration in Industrial America* (New York, 1981), 64.

37. For instance, Newark's benefit societies, which emerged as multiclass and

multicraft associations, were homogeneous ethnic organizations that cut across class lines and included employers as well as employees. Moreover, these "informal networks of friends," when in large factories, helped mitigate discontent. Hirsch, *Roots*.

38. Kivisto, among others, observes as much; and given the fact that radicalism and class militance bulked larger among Finnish immigrants than any other group of newcomers, it should surely be a valid observation for other ethnic blocs. Kivisto, 162.

39. A comparable hypothesis, and I am indebted to it, has been suggested by Carl Kaestle and Maris P. Vinovskis, *Education and Social Change in Nineteenth-Century Massachusetts* (New York, 1980), 95.

40. Eve Bank, Dan Finn, "Working Class Images of Society and Community Studies," in Stuart Hall, et al., *On Ideology* (London, 1978), 126, 127.

41. Mark Lause, "The Unwashed Infidelity: Thomas Paine and Early New York City Labor History" (unpublished MS). On republican ideology, especially in New York, see also, Staughton Lynd, "The Mechanics in New York Politics, 1774–1778," *Labor History* 5 (1964): 230, and Alfred E. Young, "The Mechanics and the Jeffersonians, 1789–1801," ibid., 249–53.

42. Howard Rock, *Artisans of the New Republic: The Tradesmen of New York City in the Age of Jefferson* (New York, 1979), 49, 192–93. Sean Wilentz has written insightfully on the subject: Wilentz, "Artisan Republican Festivals and the Rise of Class Conflict in New York City, 1788–1837," in Michael Frisch and Daniel Walkowitz, eds., *Working-Class America: Essays on Labor, Community, and American Society* (Urbana, Ill., 1983), 49 and passim. See also Alan Dawley, *Class and Community: The Industrial Revolution in Lynn* (Cambridge, Mass., 1976).

43. Wilentz, 46. On their belief in the labor theory of value, see also Paul G. Faler, *Manufacturers in the Early Industrial Revolution: Lynn 1780–1860*, (Albany, N.Y., 1981) 181, and R. S. Neale, *Class and Ideology in the 19th Century* (London, 1972), 26.

44. Alasdair Clayre, *Work and Play* (London, 1974), 99. Also illuminating are Clyde Griffen, "The 'Old' Immigration and Industrialization: A Case Study," in Richard L. Ehrlich, ed., *Immigrants in Industrial America* (Charlottesville, Va., 1977), 176, and Susan Hirsch, "From Artisan to Manufacturer," in Stuart W. Bruchey, ed., *Small Business in American Life* (New York, 1980), 87.

45. Daniel Rogers, *The Work Ethic in Industrial America, 1850–1920* (Chicago, 1978), 174–75. On the emergent division of labor, see Griffen and Griffen, 6–7. For an overview on technological changes, see Irwin Yellowitz, *The Position of the Worker in American Society, 1865–1896* (Englewood Cliffs, N.J., 1969), 9, and Mary Ryan, *Cradle of the Middle Class* (New York, 1981), e.g., 152 on the declining expectations of journeymen and apprentice shoemakers. The replacement of skilled by semiskilled, rather than entirely unskilled, labor after 1880, was customary in many industries. John Bodnar, "Immigration, Kinship, and the Rise of Working Class Realism in Industrial America," *Journal of Social History* 14, no. 1(1980): 45.

46. Wilentz, 42 and passim. The defensive character of artisanal resistance, when confronted by industrialism, is explored by Rock, 279 and passim. See also L. Schneider, 473–75.

47. Roy Rosenzweig, "'Eight Hours for What We Will': Workers and Leisure in Worcester, Massachusetts, 1870–1920" (Ph.D. diss., Harvard University, 1978).

48. David Montgomery, "The Shuttle and the Cross: Weavers and Artisans in the Kensington Riots of 1844," in Stearns and Walkowitz, *Workers*, 48–49, 56–57. Also helpful is Leonard Bernstein, "The Working People of Philadelphia from

Colonial Times to the General Strike of 1835," *Pennsylvania Magazine of History and Biography* 73 (1950): 336–39.

49. Michael Barrett, "Unity and Fragmentation: Class, Race and Ethnicity among Chicago's Packing House Workers, 1900–1922" (unpublished paper), 2; Dominic Pacyga, "Polish Workers of Chicago's South Side" (unpublished MS), 235.

50. L. Schneider, 182.

51. William Gudalunas and William G. Shade, *Before the Molly Maguires: The Emergence of the Ethno-Religious Factor in the Politics of the Lower Anthracite Region, 1844–1872* (New York, 1976). See also L. Schneider, 70–74. On the class consciousness of the East and South European immigrant steelworker, see Frank Serene, "Immigrant Steelworkers in the Monongahela Valley: Their Communities and the Development of a Labor Class Consciousness" (Ph.D. diss., University of Pittsburgh, 1979), 7.

52. George Pozzetta, *Pane e lavori, The Italian American Working Class* (Toronto, 1980), 3–5. The Italian strikers at Lawrence in 1912 were overwhelmingly women operatives. Parmet, 141.

53. Steve Fraser, "Dress Rehearsal for the New Deal," in Frisch and Walkowitz, *Working-Class America*, 228–29. Hartmut Keil, "The German Immigrant Working Class of Chicago, 1875–90: Workers, Labor Leaders and the Labor Movement," in Hoerder, *American Labor*, 169–70.

54. Eugene Miller and Gianna Panovsky, "Radical Italian Unionism: Its Development and Decline in Chicago's Men's Garment Industry, 1910–1930," (Illinois Labor History Conference paper, 9–10 October 1981), 3, 7–8.

55. Jean Hales, "The Shaping of Nativist Sentiment, 1848–1860" (Ph.D. diss., Stanford University, 1973), 117, 131–32. For an example of the division of labor and of unskilled replacing skilled labor, see Bodnar, "Immigration," 49; David Grimsted, "Riot, Strike, and Communal Consensus in Ante-Bellum Labor Relations" (unpublished paper). See also Michael Feldberg, *Philadelphia Riots of 1844* (New York, 1972), passim, and Montgomery, "Shuttle and Cross," in Stearns and Walkowitz, in *Workers*, 411–46. Montgomery's contention that a fairly clear shift from class to ethnoreligious consciousness occurred in these years is perhaps questionable. At least the two coexisted generally in American labor, and the weaver strikes—less the violence—began again soon after the 1844 riots. *Pennsylvanian*, 8 August 1846; Joseph Sills, "Diary," 28 February 1845, MSS in Pennsylvania Historical Society.

56. On the Irish and Catholics in New York State, see Whitney Cross, *The Burned-Over District* (Ithaca, 1950), especially 4–6, and John Horton et al., *A History of Northwestern New York* (New York, 1947). Irish canal labor is alluded to in a number of works, including William D. Hurd, *The Catholic Church in New England* (Boston, 1899), 596, and Bernstein, 336–39. See also Laurence A. Glasco, "Ethnicity and Social Structure: Irish, Germans, and Native Born of Buffalo, New York, 1850–1860" (Ph.D. diss., State University of New York at Buffalo, 1973), 86, 93, 226. See also, on Irish canal labor, Vera Shlakman, *Economic History of a Factory Town* (Northampton, Mass., 1935), 49. Most pre-famine Irish were Protestant, with many first going to England—where they might work as harvest hands or go into the Oldham or Lancashire textile mills. See Lawrence J. McCaffrey, *The Irish Diaspora in America* (Bloomington, Ind., 1976), 60. More than a million entered the United States between 1815 and 1845. They continued down to the end of the century, and even then fewer than 10 percent were skilled. Meagher, 118. In Jersey City, for instance, they composed 75 percent of the unskilled labor force; in Lawrence, Detroit, and Cohoes, they

were in the unskilled occupational category. Zunz, 37, finds only 0.8 percent of Irish fell into the "high white collar" category of workers in 1880 Detroit. Douglas V. Shaw, "The Making of an Immigrant City: Ethnic and Cultural Conflict in Jersey City, New Jersey, 1850–1877" (Ph.D. diss., University of Rochester, 1973).

57. Douglas Shaw carefully discusses the Irish experience in Jersey City. See also Michael Gordon, "The Labor Boycott in New York City, 1880–1886," in Milton Cantor, *American Workingclass Culture* (Westport, Conn., 1979), 287–332, for treatment of Irish working class in New York City. On rural Ireland, its society and violence, see Oliver MacDonalgh, "Irish Famine Migration," in *Perspectives in American History* 10 (1976): 384–85.

58. Thomas Dublin, *Woman at Work: The Transformation of Work and Community in Lowell, Massachusetts, 1826–1860* (New York, 1979), 155, 156.

59. The Order of United American Mechanics as late as 1905 was composed of Protestant native-born skilled workers. They supported immigrant restriction, which was not an issue in the 1830s or 1840s. The Steelton branch passed a resolution that resolved: "We demand the enactment of such laws as will shield us from the depressing effections of unrestricted immigration, to the end that the American laborer may not only be protected against the product of the foreign pauper laborer, but that we may be protected against direct competition in our own country by the incoming of the *competitive alien*—the foreign pauper laborers themselves," quoted in John Bodnar, *Immigration and Industrialization, Ethnicity in an American Mill Town, 1870–1940* (Pittsburgh, 1977), 39. Turning back some fifty years, New England's nativists—those in Massachusetts's Know-Nothing lodges, for instance—also included a disproportionate number of artisans—shoemakers, weavers, carpenters. The "vast majority" of Worcester's came out of stores and artisan shops, with 75 percent of the Know-Nothings drawn from skilled trades. Charles Buell, "The Workers of Worcester" (Ph.D. diss., New York University, 1974). On the Massachusetts Know-Nothings, see Michael Holt, "The Politics of Impatience: The Origins of Know-Nothingism," *Journal of American History* 60 (September 1973): 329. In both Newark and Jersey City the story is much the same: The town's skilled workers were largely native-born, of which many voted Know-Nothing in 1854: On Neward, see Hirsch, *Roots*, 120.

60. Dennis Clark, *The Irish in Philadelphia* (Philadelphia, 1973), chaps. 2, 4. Nativism as a reflection of change is discussed in Donald Kinzer, *Episode in Anti-Catholicism: The American Protective Association* (Seattle, 1964), 140. Racism and nativism as a reaction to the new social order is explored in Richard Weiss, "Racism in the Era of Industrialism," in Gary Nash and Richard Weiss, eds., *The Great Fear: Race in the Mind of America* (New York, 1970), 124–25. For a useful discussion of how and why immigrants were blamed for the disorganization of urban life, see Wiebe, 54–56, and Bessie L. Pierce, *A History of Chicago*, vol 3: *The Rise of the Modern City* (New York, 1957), 32–33. On early labor violence on docks and canals and railways, see Bernstein, 333–39. See also John Schneider, "Community and Order in Philadelphia, 1834–1844," *Maryland Historian* 5 (Spring 1974). On New York City riots, see Herbert Asbury, *Gangs of New York* (Garden City, N.Y., 1927); Leon Richards, *Gentlemen of Property* (New York, 1970). See also Allan Grimshaw, "Lawlessness and Violence in America," *Journal of Negro History* 44 (January 1959): 52–55. On the urban poor, see Carol Groneman, "The 'Bloody Ould Sixth': A Social History of a New York City Workingclass Community in the Mid-Nineteenth Century" (Ph.D. diss., University of Rochester, 1973), 179–80. For an illuminating discussion of the loss of community feeling in

New York City and the corollary rise of new associations, see John Schneider, "Mob Violence and Public Order in the American City, 1830–1865" (Ph.D. diss., University of Minnesota, 1971). There is a very substantial literature on nativist riots. See, for example, on the 1849 St. Louis riot (of nativist fire companies versus Irish residents along the levee), Thomas Scharf, *History of Saint Louis City and County* (Philadelphia, 1883), 2:836–37. On Know-Nothing violence see W. Darrell Overdyke, *The Know Nothing Party in the South* (Baton Rouge, La., 1950). On the Boston (Charleston) riots of 1834, see Ray Billington, "The Burning of the Charleston Convent," *New England Quarterly* 10 (June 1937): 4–24; and on the Pennsylvania antiabolitionist riot of 1830, see J. Schneider, "Mob Violence," chap. 4. On a number of antiabolitionist mobs, see Richards.

61. Adrian Cook, *The Armies of the Streets* (Lexington, Ky., 1974), 27, 29.

62. Elizabeth M. Geffen, "Violence in Philadelphia," *Pennsylvania History* 36 (October 1969): 392. See also Ray Billington, *The Protestant Crusade* (Chicago, 1964), and Thomas Scharf and Thompson Westcott, *History of Philadelphia* (Philadelphia, 1887), 1:663–68. On the 1844 riots, see Feldberg, *Philadelphia Riots*, and J. Schneider, "Community and Order in Philadelphia."

63. Robert Ernst, *Immigrant Life in New York City* (New York, 1949), 106; Grimsted, 4–5; J. Bennet Nolan, "The Battle of Womelsdorf," *Pennsylvania Magazine of History and Biography* 78 (January 1954): 361–68; Feldberg, *Philadelphia Riots*. Thus on the streets of Kensington, the battles of Ireland were replayed, an intraclass struggle between Irish Protestant and Irish Catholic handloom weavers: see Ira Harkavy, "Reference Group Theory and Group Conflict and Cohesion in Advanced Capitalist Countries: Presbyterians, Workers, and Jews in Philadelphia, 1790–1968 (Ph.D. diss., University of Pennsylvania, 1979).

64. Rudolph Vecoli, "The Formation of Chicago's 'Little Italies,'" *Journal of Ethnic History* (Spring 1983): 9–10.

65. Hirsch, *Roots*, 104–5. In Chicago, for instance, there was a bitter fight over tax monies and the Protestant Bible; in New York, in 1840, the Irish divided over the organization of a separate school system (see David Montgomery, *Beyond Equality: Labor and Radical Republicans, 1862–1872* [New York, 1962], 43, and Jay Dolan, *Catholic Revivalism* [Notre Dame, Ind., 1978], 92); in San Francisco, education became a virtual battleground between Irish and Italian working-class versus native-born Protestant workers who allied with elite reformers in the post–World War I period (Victor Shradar, "Ethnicity, Religion, and Class: Progressive School Reform in San Francisco," *History of Education Quarterly* 20 [Winter 1980]: 385–87); and in other cities, educational issues often joined with the crusade against the liquor traffic and, channeled into political alliances, further heightened social tensions. Philadelphia, for one, suffered from chronic nativist agitation that mushroomed especially after the 1837 panic but then declined by 1844. See Montgomery, "Shuttle and Cross," in Stearns and Walkowitz, *Workers*. For comparable developments and issues in New York City, see Herbert I. London, "The Nativist Movement in the American Republican Party in New York City during the Period 1843–1847" (Ph.D. diss., New York University, 1966), 38, 56, 198–200. Lee Benson, *The Concept of Jacksonian Democracy* (Princeton, 1961), also emphasizes sociocultural developments and finds an economic explanation for such developments to be too simplistic. So does Michael Feldberg in a useful survey, *The Turbulent Era: Riot and Disorder in Jacksonian America* (New York, 1980), 6–7.

For divisions between Irish Protestant and Irish Catholic, see Clark, *Irish in Philadelphia*, 21, passim; Feldberg, *Philadelphia Riots* on native-born and nativist Whigs and Irish Catholic Democrats in Pittsburgh—such as the "days of terror" that accompanied St. Patrick's Day and the Orangemen parade of 12 July. Divisions between Newark Protestant and Catholic workers over temperance are explored in Hirsch, *Roots*, 104, J. Walter Coleman, *The Molly Maguire Riots* (Ann Arbor, 1969), 19, describes anti-Catholic rioting. In Pittsburgh, Nora Faires tells us, German Catholics fought the Irish Catholic church hierarchy as well as Protestant nativists. Nora Faires, "The Evolution of Ethnicity: The German Community in Pittsburgh and Alleghany City, Pennsylvania, 1845–1885" (Ph.D. diss. University of Pittsburgh, 1982), 18. On Boston's Protestant and Catholic working-class rioting in 1837 and the 1840s, see, respectively, Michael S. Hindus, *Prison and Plantation: Crime, Justice and Authority in Massachusetts and South Carolina, 1767–1878* (Chapel Hill, N.C., 1980), and James Green and Hugh C. Donahue, *Boston's Workers: A Labor History* (Boston, 1979), 29. In Detroit, the Polish National Catholic Church sought to structure the community to ensure its religious independence from the German and Irish Catholic hierarchy, and its excommunicated members then built its own Polish Catholic church, contrary to orders from the hierarchy (Zunz, 188, 190). Victor Greene describes a comparable conflict between Poles and the Roman church hierarchy, but on this occasion the Slavic element was divided against the diocese over church control. Greene, *For God and Country: The Rise of Polish and Lithuanian Ethnic Consciousness in America, 1860–1910* (Madison, Wis., 1975), 10–13, and passim. In commenting on politics, one should also note, even in passing, another source of ethno-Catholic dispute, not necessarily limited to working-class America, namely, the election riots, such as those between Pittsburgh's native-born Whigs and Irish Catholic Democrats, or the spring melee in St. Louis, which pitted nativist against Irish and German residents. Such riots were not always inspired by purely political events. The April 1834 municipal election trouble in eastern cities, for instance, was prompted by more than Jackson's veto of the BUS recharter. It was interlaced with ethnoreligious antagonism. The Irish voted for Jackson and the Democratic Party, and the tensions were sparked by a discrete electorate as much as by political or economic issues. See J. Schneider, "Mob Violence," 58–59. On ethnic conflict as the basis of nineteenth-century political alignments, see Gudalunas and Shade, *Before the Molly Maguires*. Conversely, political solidarity followed from religious homogeneity, as in Scranton, where Irish Catholics voted solidly Democratic, while the Welsh, divided among several religious denominations, were also politically divided. Walker, 54.

66. Alan Conway, ed., *The Welsh in America* (Minneapolis, 1961), 168. On Schuylkill miners and ethnoreligious as well as political polarization in the 1840s, and its primacy for Welsh and English Protestant miners, see Gudalunas, 52, 63.

67. P. E. Gibbons, "The Miners of Scranton, Pennsylvania," *Harpers Magazine* 55 (November 1877): 923. On Welsh dominance of mining-boss ranks, see H. M. Alden, "The Pennsylvania Coal Regions," *Harpers Magazine* 227 (September 1963).

68. David Brody, *Steelworkers in America: The Nonunion Era* (Cambridge, Mass., 1960). The "massive flow" of South and East European immigrants into Steelton, for instance, dramatically increased "social divisions," John Bodnar has concluded (in *Immigration and Industrialization*, xvi).

69. W. Jett Lauck, "The Cotton Mill Operative of New England," *Atlantic Monthly* 109 (1912): 109–10. Philip Silvia, Jr., "The Spindle City: Labor, Politics and Religion in Fall Rivers, Massachusetts, 1870–1905" (Ph.D. diss., Fordham University, 1973), 8, 14.

70. John Rowe, *Hard-Rock Miners: Cornish Immigrants and the North American Mining Frontier* (New York, 1974), 247.

71. Montgomery, *Beyond Equality*, 40. For the intense hostility of cigarmaking craftsmen toward cheap Chinese labor, see Samuel Gompers, *Some Reasons for Chinese Exclusion* (Washington, 1902). Another pamphlet indicating Gompers's racism, written with Herman Gutstadt, is *Meat vs. Rice: American Manhood against Asiatic Coolieism: Which Shall Survive?* (Washington, D.C., 1901). See also Saxon Mann, "Gompers and the Irony of Racism," *Antioch Review* 12 (June 1953): 205. Finally, there is Gompers's *Seventy Years of Life and Labor* (New York, 1925), 2:1952. On the militancy of some new ethnic groups, particularly Slavic and Italian miners in Spring Valley, Illinois, in 1894, as well as in the Pennsylvania fields at this time, see Harry Barnard, *Eagle Forgotten* (New York, 1938), 276–79. These two groups of new immigrant miners and also those from Belgium spoke in terms of struggle and resorted to bloody actions in both Illinois and Pennsylvania in 1894, frequently clashing with the older miners. See also Richard Jensen, *The Winning of the Midwest* (Chicago, 1971), 254–55.

72. Albert Gedicks, "Working Class Radicalism among Finnish Immigrants in Minnesota and Michigan Mining Communities" (Ph.D. diss., University of Wisconsin, 1979), 122.

73. Tamara Hareven, *Family Time and Industrial Time* (New York, 1982), 137. "Familial obligations," Bodnar has observed of East Europeans (in *Immigration*, 55) "dominated workingclass predilections," and the workers' behavior in the workplace became "an extension of their family world" ibid., 56.

74. Serene, 58; Doyle, 217.

75. Morawska, "Internal Status Hierarchy," 80; Hareven, 85; Wyman, 43.

76. Alan Dawley, "E. P. Thompson and the Americans," *Radical History Review* 17 (Winter 1978–79): 40.

# "Ethnicity and the World of Work": A Comment

## Dennis Clark

The chief pleasure of reading Milton Cantor's paper is to find the breadth of his view in surveying the American labor experience. Indeed, I would have been even more pleased had he cast the net of his fine inquiry even further. Although it is the usual practice for those interested in labor history to delimit their inquiries to organized labor, most working people were never members of such organizations. It is a more appropriate orientation, therefore, to look first at work life as such, at the social structure of work life in the broadest sense, and then to focus on labor organization and unionization trends.

The entire vast drama of the engagement of Americans with industrialization and the reponses of ethnic groups to this drama is very helpfully delineated by Cantor. His broad portrayal of the great diffusion of ethnic groups is instructive in its geographical scope and recollection of human suffering and responses. I would only add that, if anything, his portrayal underemphasizes the inhumane and exploitative conditions to which immigrants and groups with low social status were subjected. Their responses in forming communal and organizational defenses, whether residential, occupational, religious or entrepreneurial, were exertions dedicated to survival. These defenses often were not transplantations of some European peasant or folk modalities so much as they were desperate, almost primitive attempts to gain shelter from the social and economic punishment being meted out by a highly exploitative emerging industrialism.

The disruptive effects of interethnic and interreligious conflicts and the dislocations of the shifting laboring scene did produce, as is documented richly in the paper's citations, limitations and frustrations of ethnic group efforts to maintain stability and to construct protective and adaptive socal media. The paper attributes much of this severe dislocation to ethnic rivalry and parochial issues, as well as to company utilization of ethnic conflicts. It should be recalled, however, that some of this fragmentation and disruption in worker populations was due also to the fragmented, crippled, and sticken nature of the culture of emigration and exile shared by the ethnic groups in their American settings. The emigrants bore with them broken shards as well as ancient vessels of cultural behavior. In Ireland, Poland, southern Italy, and elsewhere life was harsh, and centuries of abuse of land and people had deeply compromised the integrity of rural social and cultural traditions. Cruelty, bitterness, and antagonism were not visited on these groups only in America, and the groups were quite capable of generating their own indigenous quotients of these misfortunes. Deculturization was a reality, both in the old countries and the new, and often it left the ethnic populations in an extremely vulnerable position amid migratory and socially disorganized industrial situations.

It must be noted that much of the work life of these mobile labor populations was not involved with clearly identifiable industrial corporate forms. Rather, it was casual, scattered, often in disarray, and not what unionization was likely to organize. Railroad subcontractors recruited their own work gangs, miners formed their own pit-hole crews, laborers took whatever digging jobs were at hand. We tend for the sake of scholarly purposes to impose more order on the vast panorama than was characteristic of it. Still, it is very valuable to have Cantor's extensive framework and perspective on this subject because it highlights the fact that the ethnic contribution to the immensities of labor and industrial development was national in scope, continuous over time, and a primary, though brutalized, feature of American economic growth. This is especially evident in the case of the Irish, whose labor contribution from the 1820s through the mid twentieth century ranged through the entire array of extractive, transport, and productive processes in all areas of the country across one cycle of economic boom and bust after another. In many ways the Irish were prototypical in their involvement with industry, but in the length of their minority status and the diversity of their experience, they do appear to have been singular.

Cantor emphasizes the diversity and division of ethnic population and the way these tended to undercut class consciousness and labor-organizing efforts. His presentation of evidence in this respect and his admirable documentation is most helpful on this subject. It is, though, of considerable import for us to recognize that there were many sources of diversity and division other than ethnic loyalty and religious conflict. The basic sociological irregularity of life, the intervention of unforeseen forces, and the contradictions of work in new and unprecedented settings contributed to diversification of work life. The sheer extent of geographical spread throughout the American landscape alone accounted for differing reactions. Industry and work life itself were a congeries of ad hoc arrangements, motley structures, and jerry-built schemes for several generations. The revolutionary pace of the scramble for resources and the construction of facilities, subject to growth, change, abandonment, and rediscovery, was a source of extraordinary differentiation. These factors should remind us that even in homogeneous societies, class unity has been elusive, temporary, and limited. Not even tyrannized Marxist societies have eliminated the natural tensions and normal persistence of ethnic groups. Hence, to attribute the incompleteness of class consciousness primarily to ethnic factors is an inappropriate judgment. They were simply part of a multiplicity of factors militating against worker unity.

A fixation with class has tended to divert many observers from the wider range of influences that have intersected in the work life of industrialized labor forces. The destruction of traditional cultural patterns among immigrants, the depersonalization of life in a mass society, the irrational impact of unemployment, and the vulnerability of individuals and families in the face of massive waves of social change all contributed to a confusion of identities, loyalties, and viewpoints that undercut solidarity. Not only was class solidarity undercut, but the personalities, families, and basic social relations of workers were very often deformed, so that alcoholism, breakdown, and brooding melancholy characterized many victims of the industrial system. Tragic though European and Asian conditions were, the work world of America was frequently rampant with its own potent misfortunes.

The sources cited in this paper are of special interest because they extend so far geographically. Although citations for New England and the mid-Atlantic states predominate, western miners are also documented. The sources also indicate what we have not summarized with respect to American work life. Black and white ethnic work life in the South are not sufficiently noted. While textiles, mining, canal labor, and garment work are alluded to, railroad and port work, food processing, agricultural labor, and extensive economic areas of fabrication such as tanning, rubber manufacture, and early chemical manufacturing, each with a group of hazardous and repulsive job categories, are not documented. Each of these areas of work employed hordes of ethnic labor. It is simply an observation about how incomplete our most commonly cited references in this field are.

It is important in the light of Cantor's presentation to recognize that, even in view of the conflicts and disabilities he catalogs among ethnic groups, their interaction with American economic life was such that their presence was, and perhaps still is, indispensable to our economic development. The heritage of skills, work values, and group loyalties that they brought from other lands was a fundamental prelude to the industrial economy. Their need for advancement and status was a powerful motivating element in the dynamic of labor achievement. The institutional structures based on their family and ethnic community aggregations created America's first widespread nongovernmental vehicles of social service for those excluded from the privileged classes and access to mainstream advantages. The immensity of this historic role continues to unfold as our investigation proceeds, gradually freeing itself from the prejudicial limitations that for so long frustrated this kind of research among our learned class.

# "Ethnicity and the World of Work": A Comment

## ARTHUR B. SHOSTAK

If we are to strengthen our grasp of the multifaceted role ethnicity has played in the history of work in this country we will require the careful, exacting scholarship of the kind exemplified in Milton Cantor's essay. For with his patient and far-ranging research as our guide, we can venture the bolder type of speculation he chooses to leave to others, a reasonable division of labor in matters as complete as these.

Cantor usefully reminds us of the remarkable tension that characterized the immigrant's life at work: Adult and child alike faced primitive workplace deficiencies, unregulated class warfare between unforgiving capitalists and unbending labor organizers, rivalries of assimilated versus freshly arrived newcomers, Old World intergroup hostilities, and the horrendous roller coaster of business boom and bust. Coursing through all of this was the central question with which we still wrestle; namely, how are we to honor our ethnic origins while also celebrating our status as proud "Calvinist" achievers in the great American middle mass?

As thorough and sweeping as is the scope of Cantor's material, more might have been made of the undersung role of women workers in the relationship between work and ethnicity. Many were responsible for keeping alive their traditional ethnic rites and rituals at home, even while balancing a new role as a pro-assimilation aide in the lives of their native-born children. Many, too, were key militants in efforts to organize early labor unions, a role that obliged them to forge unprecedented alliances across ethnic barriers and to explore the relative place of ethnicity versus class.

Similarly, while the essay covers much that one would expect, and even more that is a welcome addition, the coverage of the

120

early decades of the labor movement might usefully be expanded. Particular attention is owed to the mid-nineteenth-century effort of the National Labor Union and the Knights of Labor to clarify how ethnic pride, craft pride, and class solidarity could be melded into one powerful organizing principle.

At the risk of recommending alterations that would expand an essay into a thick tome, I would also appreciate more attention to the admittedly minor, but no less fascinating, role played in the work scene by authentic ethnic variations on the theme. Specifically, the worker-owned plywood mills established by socialist Finns on the West Coast, the worker cooperatives developed by German-American immigrants to the Midwest, and the *padrone* "labor gang" system of early Italian-American immigrants in the East challenged prevailing workplace culture in a dramatic fashion.

As students of this subject are quick to acknowledge, its content and detail threaten to escape manageable control and inundate one at every turn. It is, therefore, entirely understandable to note the tight rein Cantor held on the discussion, and the hard choices he obviously made about what to emphasize and what to slight. Somewhat less understandable, and far more regrettable, was his decision not to attempt in a deliberately venturesome summary paragraph some notion of what it all has meant, some overarching insight into the living relevance of this historic record to our current quandaries. But, as I noted at the outset, others are free to shoulder this very demanding task, and they will find much of value on which to draw in Cantor's methodical and traditional account.

# 4

## *Making It in America—and in the World: The Cultural Factor*

### Michael Novak

There is a story about a minister who stood before his congregation, which, after several weeks of excessive drought, had come together to pray for rain. "You came here," the minister said, looking out over his flock, "to pray for rain. Then where are your umbrellas?" In a follow-up story, it is said that the rains came, and came, and came—until floods occurred. "We prayed for rain, Lord," one parishioner sighed, "but this is ridiculous!"

Twelve years ago when I was writing *The Rise of the Unmeltable Ethnics,* the body of materials on ethnicity in the United States amounted to only a small fraction of what is now available. After the drought, there seems to have come a flood. It is virtually impossible, even full time, to keep up with all the books and articles, surveys, and fresh historical studies that have come to light.

The papers prepared for this conference indicate how sophisticated and complex these inquiries have become. Important new distinctions are being made. Generalizations once possible before are being challenged by close empirical work. The texture of cultural life in the United States is even richer and more fascinating than anyone might have thought a decade or more ago.

Since my own disciplines are philosophy and theology, not social science, I cannot pretend to carry the knowledge and powerful methods that are second nature to those who are trained in history, sociology, anthropology, economics, and other disciplines. If there is any contribution I can still make to the discussion, it is to step back from the empirical materials in order to reflect upon the larger significance of what we seem to be accomplishing.

From now until the end of the century, many of the world's best minds are likely to become involved in the universal problem of economic development. Permit me to review briefly the long-range scenario.

In 1800, demographers say, there were about 800 million persons on this planet. That's all. Today there are about 4.4 billion. Something dramatic occurred in the world at about the end of the eighteenth century and the beginning of the nineteenth: For the first time in history, the human race hit upon the secret of creating new wealth. Until that time, the wealth of the world was considered to be finite, a zero-sum game, in which gains for some were taken only at the expense of others. Under the reigning philosophy of mercantilism, it was the purpose of state policy to acquire money, gold in particular, in excess of that of other nations. In literature, a common figure of villainy was the miser, who in his hoarding subtracted from the limited common store. The ancient biblical vision of seven lean years following upon seven fat years still seemed to reflect reality. Poverty was virtually universal. Life for the vast majority was solitary, poor, nasty, brutish, and short. An inquiry into the nature and cause of the wealth of nations—their capacity to *produce* wealth, not simply to beggar their neighbors for it—had not been imagined until the work of Adam Smith in 1776.

As Karl Marx has pointed out, the revolution articulated first by Adam Smith was the pivotal revolutionary force in history. Since that time, almost exponentially, the wealth of the earth has multiplied. Since that time, one by one, various nations of the world have entered upon the long marathon of development. One by one, new nations continue to pass various milestones in average mortality, literacy, education, per capita income, and the rest. Today, the passion for development has become universal. There is not a nation that has not shaken off its slumbers and begun to move.

Furthermore, since 1945, some 110 new nations have achieved their independence and launched a variety of experiments in political economy. Immense migrations, some voluntary, some coerced, have occurred. Populations have increased, as have per capita annual income and average annual income. Nonetheless, the pattern is most uneven. Some nations, rich in natural resources and/ or geography, have done relatively poorly; others, not particularly favored by nature, have zoomed ahead.

In studying the multiple experiments in political economy undertaken since 1945, moreover, international economists have begun to pay increasing attention to "human capital," that is, to cultural diversity. For it seems that, more than anything else, economic development depends on what happens in aggregated minds, hearts, and hands—in the array of attitudes, beliefs, skills, habits, and dispositions of individuals in cultural groups. The natural focus of social scientists, of course, is not so much upon individuals but upon cultures: upon institutionalized attitudes, beliefs, skills, habits, and dispositions. To put the point perhaps too bluntly, some cultures are better organized than others for the creation of new wealth. This was Servan-Schreiber's point in *The American Challenge* (1968), in which he pointed out that even France, in relation to the United States, had not sufficiently organized itself around practical intellect, the source of wealth. Those cultures, he argued, that are better organized for invention, intellect, and practical creativity would be the wealth-producers of the future. Those less well organized would suffer by comparison. Some cultures are "making it," others are not.

In short, many of the comparative studies that students of ethnicity within the United States have been conducting have universal bearing. Different cultures, it appears, do tend to prepare their members differently for various social achievements, not solely in the field of economics but also in many others. To be born into a family of a certain sort, even into a religion of a certain sort, even into a set of cultural institutions of a certain sort, does tend to provide individuals with differentiated social skills of many kinds. Many such skills have economic consequences. Others have consequences for other phases of human life.

In such matters, there need be no invidiousness. One does not have to say that one culture is "better" or "superior" or "more developed" than another, in some absolute sense. Depending on the measures employed, each may have human advantages lacking in others. It is only when attention focuses on a culture's aptitude for development in political economy that a more narrow standard is applied, as when one speaks of the "developed," "less developed," and "least developed" countries. In these terms, no one denies that nations "least developed" in, say, economic skills may be more highly developed in certain facets of spirituality, wisdom, a sense of tragedy or humor, or in other most valuable human qualities. Humans do not live by bread alone. It is the universal desire for bread, however, that leads attention to be focused on the more narrow gate of economic development.

Permit me here to use a homely example. I have often noted my own ignorance and inability in something I much admire: the ability to launch a successful business. (My personal fantasy is to be the owner of a wine store.) How would one go about it, and not lose one's shirt? Once I asked a young neighbor of mine, who had just opened a pizza parlor on a beach strip surrounded by competitors, how he had the courage to risk his savings in such a (to me) unlikely venture. He smiled, twenty-five years of age as he was, and said he was already planning to add 200 square feet as soon as the season closed. He said his father owned nine restaurants, in which he himself had worked in every position and taken inventory and managed accounts since reaching the age of ten. He said it was his ambition to own at least five restaurants by the time he was thirty-five.

It seemed to me that this young man had received through his family—for all I know, extending back several generations—what I think I could never acquire. To him launching a business, creating wealth, was second nature, to me an almost insurmountable barrier. The skills he had learned since the age of ten constitute human capital of a sort lacking to me. It struck me, too, that much of his human capital was inherited through his family and, perhaps, in some measure through the mercantile culture into which he had luckily been born.

Whatever the merits of this example, I want now to draw attention to several important lines of inquiry. First, what do we know about human capital? Can anyone analyze those attitudes, beliefs, skills, habits, and dispositions (the "second nature") that are more likely than others to lead to the production of new wealth?

Second, what do we know about "political economy"? That is, are there some systems, some institutionalized ideas, that are more favorable than others to the success of persons endowed with the required human capital? Thomas Jefferson designed the seal of the United States to bear the inscription *Novus ordo seclorum,* "the new *order* of the ages." This was first an idea, and *ordo,* a system. The contemporary world is witness to some 160 different national experiments in political economy. There are 160 *ordines* or systems. What do we know about how these 160 compare in creativity, productivity, distribution, fairness, and the like? Intuitively, it seems obvious that even persons highly developed in their personal human capital may be frustrated by living within a system of political economy badly designed for their own striving. Contrariwise, it seems obvious that some systems of political economy nourish and draw out from their participants resources of human capital that might otherwise lie fallow and undeveloped.

Third, to what extent is human capital imitable, transferable, teachable? In other words, can the various components of human capital be taught? If so, what lesson plan would be the most efficient and successful? For, surely, if we know how to educate persons in the requirements of human capital, we would greatly increase their economic creativity, inventiveness, and productivity.

Fourth, there is a contemporary prejudice that education in school is the shortest route to developing human capital. But is this so? It is likely to seem so to those of us who teach. That is, in at least a limited sense, one of our main raisons d'être. And, no doubt, literacy, the ability to make distinctions, to reason in certain ways, to compute, to imagine, and to inquire, can be taught in school. Yet are there other requirements of human capital that can best be taught outside of school? If so, where and how? In the family? Through the media and other institutions of image and motivation, such as the churches, associations of various kinds, seminars, and workshops? And how? Human capital suggests massive, culture-wide pursuit of "self-improvement." Of what kinds?

For various reasons, there seem to be widespread prejudices among persons trained in the liberal arts and in the social sciences against self-improvement in the fields of commerce and industry. We tend, I think, to value political activism and cultural activism more highly than we value economic activism. Perhaps we don't understand economic activism very well, and even have a certain disdain for it. It is clearly true that we value the "free market of ideas" and protect the liberties of thought and speech so important to us more fiercely than we value the "free market of economic activities" and protect the liberties of production and distribution important to economic activists. No doubt there are important reasons for these priorities, including rather more than self-interested reasons having to do with our own turf. It is, nonetheless, observable that we do leap to defend the liberty of moral transactions between consenting adults, while leaping to regulate *economic* transactions between consenting adults. To use Irving Kristol's remark, we tend to wink at adults making love on a public stage, censorious only about paying them a minimum wage.

My point here is not to reopen the ancient argument between libertarians and democratic socialists; in any case, I am not myself a libertarian. I hold that the political system and the moral-cultural system play important roles in checking and regulating the economic system. My point is, rather, that we need to examine more closely our own fundamental beliefs and practices about the subject matter in which we are engaged. That subject matter, as I understand it, is the comparative achievement of cultural groups and cultural institutions in developing human capital. We want people, all people everywhere, to make it. We recognize that they commonly do so not as individuals but as inheritors of group skills and memories. Well, then, how do various ethnic groups, both here in the United States and around the world, compare in the various measures of economic success, in wealth and in poverty, in home ownership and in education, in per capita income and in economic status? Our studies on these matters depend very much upon our own fundamental understanding of and attitudes toward the achievements we intend to measure.

There is an enormous temptation in the Zeitgeist operative during out lifetimes to study such matters through the lens of "victimization." Occasionally, studies in our field seem predicated on the principle of greater victimhood ("X is more victimized than thou"), as if every person should receive at birth a number carried out to eight digits in the quotient of victimhood each group has experienced during the last one thousand years. The difficulty into which this prejudice abuts in economic matters is well known. Not untypically, groups otherwise the victims of discrimination often demonstrate superior economic skills. In studying human capital, cultural victimhood is often far less significant than many other factors. These other factors need to be identified.

These four questions need far better answers than are now available if we are to tackle the great international and national

questions of economic development. In particular, scholars need
to probe more than they have—and with greater openness, less
hostility—into the secrets of the commercial and the industrial
arts. What actually constitutes, analytically, human capital? What
constitutes a system of political economy favorable to economic
development? What are the most efficient, institutionalized methods of self-improvement in human capital, whether for individuals or for groups? Even among groups victimized by
discrimination, whether as a caste or as a pariah group or as a race
(as Jews, Italians, and others were once thought in America to be
of inferior race), what factors led some to make magnificent advances while others remain relatively dependent and passive?

If we could give better answers than we now have to those four
questions we would be in a stronger position to identify poten-
tially creative reforms in our own systems (economic, political,
and moral-cultural), both within the United States and within
many other nations still struggling toward the ideal of development. What works? What clearly doesn't work? What really em-
powers peoples to become economic activists and what actually
holds them back?

The papers prepared for this conference shed useful light on
specific problems within this context. What it seems to me we
gradually need to devise is a larger theory of economic development useful not only for every single culture represented within
our own multicultural society but also for all the cultures on this
planet. Further attention to all the many components of human
capital, and to the institutions that nourish or impede its development, might enable us gradually to formulate a theory adequate
to the nature of development itself. Both within our own nation
and among the nations of the world, culture differs from culture
as "star differs from star in glory." In trying to figure out how each
culture can advance in human capital, we aim to heighten, not to
diminish, the glory of each. In this regard, there are some specific
points in the papers presented at this conference that I would like
to address.

First, some scholars seem to have as their fundamental intellectual aim to focus above all else on the situation of blacks in the
United States. Their work tries to show that whatever categories of
analysis are introduced, lessons that apply to all or most other
groups do not apply to blacks. They are fertile in inventing new

theories for this purpose. They have abandoned "class" as a useful tool. They are obliged to note that southern-born blacks are of typically different culture from northern-born blacks; that West Indian blacks show a remarkably different statistical profile from American-born blacks; that African-born blacks are different yet again. Still, they want to deny that "ethnicity" or "cultural pluralism" has any relevance to blacks. Recently, they have turned to "caste," "pariah status," and "structural expectation." They resort to every ingenuity to explain why the statistical profile of American-born blacks is what it is.

Why do they all do this? Their recommendations are always the same. They cannot deny the statistical profile. What they, therefore, set out to do is to show (a) that blacks must be uniquely treated as victims unable to be given responsibility for their own statistical profile; (b) that massive government interventions—through broad welfare programs, affirmative action legislation and the like—are both the only practical solution and the only moral one; and (c) that the underlying cause for this statistical profile is the racism of whites.

Let us suppose that all this is true, although many scholars and activists do not think it is. The whole picture is depressingly derogatory toward blacks. It places them in a category discriminated from all other cultural groups. It deprives blacks of any internal sources of potency, responsibility, and effectuality. It views blacks as uniquely dependent. It is, one would think, insufferably patronizing. Yet, clearly, all this is done with pure intentions. Indeed, those who do it are supremely confident of their own superior morality. It is the others, they claim, who are the racists.

Well, let us accept their vision for a moment. What is its operational effect? Their practical proposals always involve a form of state management of the affairs of blacks, a sort of socialism for blacks. It is apparent that many who hold this theory are, in fact, democratic socialists. In blacks, they seem to have the nearest moral equivalent to an exploited group—not quite a class (empirical realities will not permit that), but rather a "caste," a "pariah group."

Even accepting all this, we surely know enough from world affairs to ask: What are the most probable results of socialist methods upon their intended beneficiaries? A majority of this planet's political economies are self-declared socialist regimes in one form or another. By now, there is an empirical track record. Judgment need no longer be surrendered to wishful thinking. Probable outcomes can be predicted and tested.

The underlying statistical profiles suggest that blacks in Miami are not making it, compared with Cubans; that blacks in Newark are not making it, compared with Koreans; that in school black youngsters are not making it, compared with recent immigrants from Asia, whether Chinese, Japanese, Taiwanese, Korean, or Vietnamese; that American-born blacks do not make it, compared with immigrant West Indian blacks. Even if we look at years of educations completed, closer inspection does not allow one to observe that blacks with the same years of schooling have grades as high or skills as sharp as other cultural groups with whom they graduate. These facts need some explanation. More important, such facts need—and, evidence shows, they are highly susceptible to—dramatic correction. Certain types of schooling, and family involvement in education, do release immense capabilities in those black youngsters lucky enough to benefit by them, whether in private schools or in the high-standards, disciplined, family-involved public schools.

Moreover, home ownership helps a great deal; capital formation within families is a crucial element in family progress. So also does increased economic activism in starting businesses. Economic independence—working for oneself rather than depending upon others to provide jobs—is a sure index of growing economic power. There are 15 million small businesses in the United States, which during the 1970s produced nearly 80 percent of all new jobs (13 million of 17 million). It is in starting such businesses that the Cubans, Koreans, Vietnamese, Japanese, Chinese, and other immigrants of the 1970s are rapidly making it in America today, as did the Greeks, Italians, Armenians, Jews, and Lebanese of the pre-World War II era.

Why do so high a proportion of members of the newest immigrant groups seem to know how to start and to succeed in small businesses, while so high a proportion of American blacks seem not to do so? One needs to compare savings rates, capital accumulation rates, in cultural groups. One would also have to compare how families, whole families, capitalize their labor by contributing three or more members to a family restaurant, snack bar, tobacco shop, laundry, lawn service, or barber shop. Walter Williams makes some trenchant points in *The State against Blacks* about new government bars to entry into such fields, but even he does not explain how so many immigrant groups of the 1970s are hurdling over these bars.

In a word, even assuming their worst-case analysis to be true (and I do not, except for purposes of argument), many scholars, it seems to me, pay too little attention to economic activism—to what its ingredients are, to how to stimulate it, and to how to provide the skills it requires. Their first waking thoughts are of the state, and when they go to bed at night they still seem to dream about the state. This is not the path to making it, here or anywhere.

Second, some scholars still miss the difference between the old ethnicity and the new. In the mobile, open, dynamic processes of a democratic capitalist political economy, it would be naive to expect ethnicity to maintain the forms of village life whence so many immigrants have derived. Ethnicity in such a society as ours retains remarkable and surprising vitality precisely because it has evolved into a new form. It is, today, carried on not so much by the intense group life of the past but by individual efforts at self-understanding and self-appropriation. One need not be less of a Jew because one teaches at any Ivy League university with mainly gentile colleagues, neighbors, and friends; nor need an Italian, Lebanese, Slovak, or Chinese lose all sense of history, place, and emotional self-understanding by living outside an ethnic ghetto. The old ethnicity tended to be parochial; the new ethnicity is—as we in this room surely are—cosmopolitan. Those who persist in seeing ethnicity as atavistic confidently predict its doom. Misunderstanding its subtlety, overlooking its spiritual habits, they miss its enduring power and capacities for self-transformation.

Third, some scholars misapprehend the nature of the American economy. Bewitched by Marx, they believe that the impersonality of the market dissolves all social bonds, corrodes family and ethnic ties, and leaves individuals solitary, atomic, and alienated. Those who worry about ethnicity as atavistic and group consciousness as racist ought to be pleased by this vision. All bad things should dissolve along with the good. But they really do not believe this. Despite themselves, they attribute immense force to at least some cultural factors, which only the militant power of the state can overcome. Rejecting the view of Thomas Sowell and

Milton Friedman and Walter Williams, that the market truly is impersonal, they also reject Marx. They hold that certain cultural factors do, alas, persist: "The heritage of slavery" and "a history of discrimination" and "racism," for example. They themselves invariably appeal to cultural factors, but only those negative ones that support their drive for greater state power.

Thus, we are all culturalists now. No one can escape the overwhelming array of facts that show the difference that being an heir to one culture, rather than another, shapes in an individual. For human beings are social animals, historical animals, symbolic animals—not mere atomic individuals. In free and pluralistic societies individuals are free to make as much or as little of their particular cultural heritages as they choose. What they cannot do is choose their own grandparents. Those whose families prepared them well for the future, during the long years of childhood and adolescence before they assumed the power of choosing for themselves, inherit priceless spiritual capital. They are incalculably lucky. If they have any gratitude at all, they try to teach their children at least as well as—one hopes, a little better than—they were taught. Thus is spiritual capital, a set of habits, skills, attitudes, manners, and dispositions, passed on through generations.

The family is nature's own vehicle of tradition; tradition is the passing along, with increments and losses, with transformations and fascinating new turns, of human capital. It is not so easy as some think to pass along social status or worldly success; the children of many talented, well-placed people in our generation are experiencing, in worldly terms, downward mobility. They are not necessarily lesser human beings on that account. Moreover, the downward mobility of some is a necessary condition for the rise of new elites from among the ranks of yesterday's poor, hungry, lean, and hardheaded children. John Adams once said that his generation fought a revolution so that their sons could prosper by farming in peace, so that their sons could be poets. This progression allowed for someone else's sons to become generals, someone else's to become farmers, and someone else's to become the new poets as the old left poetry for Hollywood. The beauty of a free society is downward mobility as well as upward, and ambitions for beauty and the arts as well as for economic independence.

Human capital is not only the secret to making it in economic development, but also the secret to the passing on of music, aesthetic judgment, religious questioning, moral growth, and the life of the human spirit. One of the best features of a social-market economy—or, as I prefer, democratic capitalism—is that it allows for cultural pluralism and avidly promotes achievement not only in the arts but in every field of the human spirit. Great cultural institutions thrive here, and ethnic traditions in the arts—like those of the Germans and the Jews in music and those of the Italians in opera—inherit both the liberty and the independent resources required to flourish mightily.

Humans do not live by bread alone. In particular, ethnicity does not. But economic activism does create the wherewithal by which liberty expresses itself in ever new forms. Human capital is simply another way of saying tradition, not a static but a dynamic, self-transforming tradition, as befits free peoples. And "making it" is simply another way of saying that groups, like individuals, can and do achieve their fullest possibilities.

The dream of Adam Smith was that the whole world, all nations, would make it. Our researches into the cultural factor in economic development in the United States have bearing on analogous cultural factors in every other nation on this planet. The task we inherit with our tradition—our own human capital—is to help to place a firm material base under every nation on this planet, so that from realistic revolution, from farming, and from industry, poetry might come.

# Conclusion

### M. MARK STOLARIK

Scholarly conferences rarely attract the attention of America's press. Seldom does one read about the deliberations of the three thousand individuals who meet during the annual convention of the Organization of American Historians or the five thousand who may attend the national gathering of the American Historical Association.

And yet, when only seventy-five people attended a two-day conference on "Making It in America" at the Balch Institute in Philadelphia, the event was reported both by the local and national press. *The New York Times, The Philadelphia Inquirer,* and the *Philadelphia Daily News* covered it extensively. This conference had obviously struck a nerve.[1]

We should not have been surprised. "Making it" (or "getting ahead") has been the underlying theme of American history since Europeans started coming to North America. Most of the passengers on the first trip to Jamestown, Virginia, in 1607 were not religious refugees but adventurers in search of their "fortunes." Even the Puritans, who did come for religious reasons, were sent by a joint-stock company that expected a return on its investment. America, then, was the "Promised Land" where people could flee to escape centuries-old laws and regulations that hindered social mobility. Here one could "make it," if only one tried.[2]

In the almost four hundred years of our national existence some groups have prospered in this country, but others have not. Those who came first (the English) had a decided advantage over those who came later. In addition, those who were already here (the Indians) and those who were brought here as slaves (Afro-Americans) were put at a disadvantage by the conquerors and masters. But now that everyone is equal before the law, can all groups prosper equally?

As the authors and commentators whose papers are presented here have shown, there is no agreement on this matter. Ivan Light finds that certain Asian groups, reacting to discrimination against them, have done spectacularly well because they marshaled their collective cultural resources to launch entrepreneurial businesses through which they successfully overcame all kinds of discrimination. David Hogan, on the other hand, argues that until recent times a "caste system," which evolved from the American slave system, prevented blacks from getting ahead through education, no matter how hard they tried. And Milton Cantor shows that, to a certain extent, the family and ethnic neighborhood institutions sheltered immigrant workers from the worst abuses of uncontrolled industrialism.

While Light, Hogan, and Cantor have made good beginnings in dealing with the subject of "making it in America," much remains to be done. As Mark Hutter and Henry Drewry pointed out, more research needs to be conducted on ethnic groups other than American blacks and Jews, who represent the two extremes when it comes to social mobility. The most noticeable omission in David Hogan's paper is any discussion of the value of education as perceived by black newspaper editors. Which leader did Afro-American editors prefer, Booker T. Washington or W. E. B. DuBois? Did the editors favor accommodation to existing conditions or demand immediate equality? Did the editors believe that education did, indeed, promote social mobility, as Hogan assumes, or did they regard it as a frill with no real value? The statistics presented by Hogan do not answer these questions.

I raise this issue because in my study of the attitudes of Slovak-Americans toward education in the period 1870 to 1930, I found widespread indifference, if not hostility, toward public schooling. Slovak editors recalled that Hungary had used public schools to assimilate Slovak children into Magyar culture and denounced these institutions in America as well. Both Catholic and Lutheran leaders looked upon education (in a parochial school) not as a vehicle for social mobility but as a means of social control. Schools were places where children were supposed to be inculcated with moral and national values. "Getting ahead" was left to the workplace—in the coal mines and steel mills for men and in textile factories for women.[3]

Furthermore, all the articles in this book present a particular group's perceptions in a static way. Culture changes over time. What a group may perceive to be a frill (education) in the 1890s, it may regard as a necessity in the 1980s. Large numbers of Slovak-Americans, for example, *do* value education today and, for the first time, are sending their children to universities. Can it be that blacks, for whom education had little value in the marketplace before the 1950s, similarly adjusted to changing perceptions of the value of education over the last one hundred years? Although this question seems to be crucial to the concept of "pedagogical exchange" used by Hogan, he does not fully explore it.

Ivan Light's paper is also too present oriented, dealing with only one generation. As Randall Miller and Kenneth Kusmer point out, Light should have put his story of Korean success into historical perspective, and he should have looked at more than one generation of entrepeneurs.

Milton Cantor, by contrast, thoroughly surveys the complex and varied experiences of American workers of different ethnic backgrounds in the nineteenth century but he fails to draw any real conclusion. Cantor, and to a lesser extent Hogan, typify a peculiarity of American history—an overemphasis on historiography and an underemphasis on original research. There is no question that Cantor and Hogan are au courant with regard to historical literature, but one wonders how many diaries, newspapers, minute books, jubilee books, and other primary sources they have used to construct their histories. There is an unfortunate tendency among American historians to focus on each other's work to the detriment of original research, and this may lead to their perpetuating all kinds of assumptions (about the value of education, for instance) that may be incorrect.

Michael Novak's philosophical treatise reflects the dissatisfaction of one intellectual with American historical scholarship. He finds contemporary scholars too blinded by class and caste theories to see reality properly. Novak's essay illustrates that, if American scholars are to convince anyone of the soundness of their arguments, they will have to make better arguments.

I would second Novak's call for better arguments because of their importance for social policy. If scholars wish federal, state, and local governments to pursue more effective social policies, then scholars should ground their cases upon solid documentary evidence and present them in clear, effective English, free from jargon. Moreover, researchers should not be afraid to address the question "If one group is more successful in 'getting ahead' than another, can the latter learn from the former and get ahead as well?" As the papers presented in this book illustrate, there is at present no agreement on the answer. We hope, however, that these essays will stimulate others to ask, and try to answer, the question and thereby promote a greater awareness and understanding among all Americans of the complexity of our multicultural society. The results of such research might even rub off on our political leaders, who may, as a result, pass more enlightened social legislation for the greater good of all.

## Notes

1. William Robbins, "'Making It in America' Forum Hears of Risk in Blending of Ethnic Groups," *The New York Times*, 23 April 1983; Terry Bevins, "Are Some Ethnic Traits Entrepreneurial Gifts?" *The Philadelphia Inquirer*, 24 April 1983; Carol Towarnicky, "Ethnicity Is No Joke," *Philadelphia Daily News*, 25 April 1983.

2. Sigmund Diamond, "From Organization to Society: Virginia in the Seventeenth Century," in Stanley N. Katz, ed., Colonial America: Essays in Politics and Social Development (Boston, 1971), 4–31; Clarence L. Ver Steeg, *The Formative Years: 1607–1763* (New York, 1964), 35–39.

3. M. Mark Stolarik, "Immigration, Education, and the Social Mobility of Slovaks, 1870–1930," in Randall M. Miller and Thomas D. Marzik, eds., *Immigrants and Religion in Urban America* (Philadelphia, 1977), 103–16.

# Notes on Contributors

MILTON CANTOR (Ph.D., Columbia) is Professor of History at the University of Massachusetts, Amherst. A former editor of *Labor History*, he has published a large number of books and articles in scholarly and popular journals, including *The Divided Left* (1978) and *American Workingclass Culture* (1979).

DENNIS CLARK (Ph.D., Temple) is Executive Director of the Samuel S. Fels Foundation in Philadelphia. Formerly with the Philadelphia Commission on Human Relations, Clark has published eight books, including *Cities in Crisis* (1960) and *The Ghetto Game* (1963).

HENRY N. DREWRY (M.A., Columbia Teacher's College) is Professor and Director of Teacher Preparation at Princeton University. A coauthor (with Frank Freidel) of *America: A Modern History of the United States* (1970) and *America Is* (1982), Drewry received the Distinguished Secondary School Teacher Award from Harvard University in 1964.

MURRAY FRIEDMAN (Ph.D., Georgetown) is Middle Atlantic States Director of the American Jewish Committee and Adjunct Lecturer of the American Jewish experience at St. Joseph's University. He has published many articles in scholarly and popular journals as well as several books, including *Overcoming Middle Class Rage* (1971) and *The Utopian Dilemma, American Jews and Public Policy* (1985).

DAVID HOGAN (Ph.D., Illinois) is Associate Professor of History in the Graduate School of Education at the University of Pennsylvania and Director of the Philadelphia History of Education Project. He has published a number of articles on the social history of American education and a book on *Class and Reform: School and Society in Chicago, 1880–1930* (1985).

MARK HUTTER (Ph.D., Minnesota) is Associate Professor of Sociology at Glassboro State College in Glassboro, New Jersey. He has published many articles in scholarly journals and is the author of *The Changing Family: Comparative Perspectives* (1981).

KENNETH L. KUSMER (Ph.D., Chicago) is Associate Professor of History at Temple University. Among his many scholarly publications is *A Ghetto Takes Shape: Black Cleveland, 1870–1930,* which was named "Outstanding Academic Book" by *Choice* magazine in 1977, and a 1973 essay on organized charity in Chicago in the *Journal of American History* that won the Louis Pelzer Memorial Award for best essay submitted that year.

IVAN LIGHT (Ph.D., Berkeley) is Professor of Sociology at the University of California in Los Angeles. A leading expert on ethnic enterprise in America, Light has published two books and more than a dozen articles on this subject. As a supplement to his *Ethnic Enterprise in America* (1972) he is preparing for publication two more books: *Illegal Enterprise in America* and *Immigrant Entrepreneurs.*

RANDALL M. MILLER (Ph.D., Ohio State) is Professor of History at St. Joseph's University in Philadelphia and Chairman of the Academic Advisory Council of the Balch Institute. A specialist on the American South, Miller is the author or editor of eight books and more than thirty articles. He is best known for *"Dear Master":  Letters of a Slave Family* (1978) and *The Kaleidoscopic Lens: How Hollywood Views Ethnic Groups* (1980).

MICHAEL NOVAK (M.A., Harvard) is Resident Scholar at the American Enterprise Institute for Public Policy Research in Washington. Author of twenty books and more than one hundred articles in both scholarly and popular journals, he is best known for *The Rise of the Unmeltable Ethnics* (1972) and *The Spirit of Democratic Capitalism* (1982). He recently served as the United States delegate to the United Nations Human Rights Commission in Geneva.

ARTHUR B. SHOSTAK (Ph.D., Princeton) is Professor of Sociology at Drexel University. He has written or edited ten books and eighty articles in various scholarly journals, including *America's Forgotten Labor Organization* (1962) and *Blue Collar Stress* (1979).

M. Mark Stolarik (Ph.D., Minnesota) is President of the Balch Institute for Ethnic Studies in Philadelphia and Associate Director of the Temple University–Balch Institute Center for Immigration Research. Author of three books and more than twenty articles on immigration and ethnicity, as well as producer of a film, he recently published *Growing Up on the South Side: Three Generations of Slovaks in Bethlehem, Pennsylvania, 1880–1976* (1985).

# Index